How to Start and Run Your Own Shop

P. Levene

Graham & Trotman

A member of the Kluwer Academic Publishers Group
LONDON/DORDRECHT/BOSTON

First published in 1985
Second edition published in 1988

Graham & Trotman Limited
Sterling House
66 Wilton Road
London SW1V 1DE
UK

Graham & Trotman Inc.
Kluwer Academic Publishers Group
101 Philip Drive
Assinippi Park
Norwell, MA02061
USA

© P. Levene, 1985, 1988

British Library Cataloguing in Publication Data

Levene, P.
  How to start and run your own shop.
  1. Stores, Retail—Great Britain—Management
  I. Title
  381'.1'0941   HF5429.6.G7

  ISBN 1-85333-107-4
  ISBN 1-85333-033-7

Typeset in Great Britain by Bookworm Studio Services, Salford
Printed and bound in Great Britain by Adlard & Son Ltd, Letchworth, Herts

Contents

v

Offices, Shops & Railway Premises Act 1963 •
Accidents at Work • Trading Standards Department •

Foreword

If a shopkeeper, or a prospective shopkeeper, wishes to buy a book written about shops, he will find that the majority of them refer to 'small businesses' and are written by accountants. When he reads one of these books, he will find that the 'small businesses' referred to may be mail order firms, small factory units, items produced from home, guest houses, window cleaning rounds, etc., etc. They are written in generalisations, by people who may be qualified to tell you how to keep your books, but not how to cope with the day-to-day problems that beset a shopkeeper.

This book fills that gap. It is aimed at the people who run, or are thinking of running, a retail shop. All the information in this book is pertinent. It was a labour of love, written during an enforced lay-off period between shops: an occupational hazard.

I was waiting for a shop to be built for me, having sold my own in time to give me a couple of months break, and was then told the building work on the new shop would be delayed by a further three months. I took this opportunity to collect together all the snippets of information and scraps of paper I had sorted away for myself which contained useful details I might need some day, and decided to amalgamate them all into a book which would prove invaluable not only to newcomers to retailing, but also to experienced shopkeepers like myself. Even before the book was finished I found I had cause to refer to various sections to settle arguments as to the 'rights' of various friends and relations who were involved in retail trades.

I also found that having the time to think about each aspect of a shop at length, helped to bring to the surface the stored knowledge one has, and made me realise that there were various things I could have done to try to improve my last shop whilst there.

If you are a shopkeeper already, I know you will benefit from the 'Rules and Regulations' chapter, and feel sure that the rest of the book will act as a mental stimulant for the improvement of your business.

If you are thinking of buying a shop for the first time — you cannot do without it.

For those of you who wish to gain practical experience in the running of a shop, and want to find out if you are actually suited to such a life, we have started a series of retailing courses in real life situations. This is an ideal way to 'test the water' before actually going ahead with a purchase and committing yourself financially. Details may be found on page 182.

Reference has been made in the book to 'Bloggs Sausages', and examples given using this name. I would like to state that I know of no firm of sausage makers called Bloggs, but just in case there is one, I have created a monthly accounting and delivery system for them, which I am certain will ensure the fictitiousness of the suggested company.

This is not meant to imply that sausages should only be bought once a month — far from it!

Peter Levene

PART 1

Trading as . . .

Introduction

I am not going to spend too much time on this subject as I believe it to be of minor importance, and much better explained to you by your accountant. He will give you the best advice after reviewing all your particular circumstances.

You can trade as a:

(1) Sole Trader

This is where a shop is owned by an individual, and trades as such. The main advantages are that you own the shop, make all the decisions, and are not accountable to anyone else as long as you do not break the law. Another advantage is the simplicity with regard to your accountants. The main disadvantage is that if you get into financial trouble your own personal possessions and assets may be sold to pay off your creditors. This, of course, would only be as a last resort, and if a business is properly investigated initially, and subsequently looked after, there is no reason why this should even be considered. Another disadvantage is the fact that if you earn a lot of money one year, you pay a lot of tax, and if you make a loss the following year, you will probably not be able to claim back any of the tax paid from the previous year. However, in by far the majority of shops, the yearly difference in trade and net profit will not vary tremendously, and this second disadvantage will not have any great significance.

(2) Partnership

All the advantages and disadvantages of the 'sole trader' apply, except that in this case any decisions as to general policies, profit margins, salaries, etc. must be made with the co-operation of the partner(s). As a general principle I do not agree with having partners — there can be too many headaches. If you must, then have a Deed of Partnership drawn up legally to cover all eventualities even if you are going into

1

business with your most trusted friend. The only exception to this is if your partner is your wife.

Occasionally it may be necessary to take a partner because of an asset he has, which you badly need — such as money or expertise. In these circumstances it is best to make sure that you each fully understand what is expected of you, and agree with the designation of all duties, because if you cannot agree beforehand, I would not give much for your future, and there is very little chance of the partnership lasting for any length of time. Ask each other whatever questions you have any doubts about, and then decide how you would feel about leaving the other in charge if you were away for any length of time. This is perhaps the most pertinent question — would you trust him? Do not take a chance and begin trading with the attitude "We'll have a go, and see how it works out". There may be some of his money in the business, but there is also YOURS, and if the partnership goes down, so will your money.

The following points are possible areas of contention, and should be resolved before trading begins.

(a) Are you agreed on your choice of bank, accountant, and solicitor?
(b) Will business cheques need both partners' signatures?
(c) Have you agreed on the amount of money each partner is putting in, and the division of the profits?
(d) How much time will be spent in the business by each partner?
(e) What about holidays?
(f) What if one of the partners wants to get involved in another business?
(g) What will be the procedure for taking on and dismissing staff?
(h) Can new partners be brought in?
(i) What will be the procedure if one of the partners wishes to leave, becomes ill, retires, or dies?
(j) How will a disagreement between the partners be resolved?

One final word. Normally each partner is legally liable for all the debts of a partnership. So, if one partner fails to pay his share, the creditors can look to the other partner to meet it. Take care!

(3) Limited Company

There are two kinds of limited companies, those which are public, and those which are private. Public companies are those which have their share prices quoted on the stock exchange, and which the public can buy and sell, such as ICI, GEC, Ford, Debenhams, etc. The shares of private companies cannot be purchased in this manner; they will usually be held by you and your wife, or partner, if you have one. The company itself is regarded as a separate entity, and any debts incurred by it will not be passed on to you, and your own personal assets will not be touched.

You cannot hold one hundred per cent of the shares yourself, but you could have 99 per cent, and your wife the other one per cent. Alternatively, if you were in an equal partnership you could have 50 per cent each. In other words, at least two people are needed, one to be the company chairman and the other to be the company secretary. The registered office of the company need not be in your place of business; in fact a better place, in my opinion, is at your accountant's office, so that all correspondence will be sent direct there, without bothering you.

A company is obviously more complicated to set up, and is governed by two sets of rules called the 'Memorandum of Association', and the 'Articles of Association'. The Memorandum is a document which sets out the main objects for which the company has been formed, and usually contains a clause making these objects as wide as possible, because it is very difficult to alter them at a later date. The Articles define the procedure for issuing shares, voting, auditing, transferring shares, etc. Before the company can exist legally, a Certificate of Incorporation must be obtained from the Registrar of Companies, and is your licence to start trading. All your stationery must have the name of the Company and the address of the registered office, your registration number, and the names of the directors. Incidentally, if the objects of the company cover too wide a field, they may not be counted as valid in a court of law.

The advantages are, as already stated, that you cannot be held personally responsible for any debts incurred by the business, and also any tax profits or losses may be carried forward to future years, thus ensuring a minimum of income tax is paid overall.

The disadvantages are that you have to send a copy of your audited accounts to the Registrar of Companies each year, and these, together with other various documents, may be inspected by any member of the public. Therefore, anyone is able to check on the names and addresses of the directors, and the size of your nominal capital, to find out if your company is sound. The company will also have to pay Corporation Tax.

If you form a company through a solicitor it will probably be very expensive. Another means of obtaining a company is by purchasing a ready-made one from a broker. This will still cost quite a few pounds, but substantially less than having one formed specially for you by a solicitor. Brokers advertise in the national press and speciality papers such as *Dalton's Weekly* and *Exchange and Mart*.

Finding the Site . . .

One of the best positions for any shop is a monopoly one in the High Street or in a densely populated urban area. Unfortunately there are very few unopposed High Street positions, especially with the advent of the modern supermarket, and although those in good secondary positions can be found, care should be taken that there are no plans for superstores or hypermarkets to be built in the surrounding areas. There is no set rule as to which type of location is generally best, be it High Street, town centre, secondary position, urban, or shopping precincts. Shops in business districts, or adjacent to factory estates, are generally well worthwhile. They have the advantage of having most of their trade concentrated into a five-day week, during normal hours, and are usually dead at weekends, and after 5.30 p.m. at night. Their disadvantages are that the trade will fluctuate according to the number of people currently employed locally, and also will suffer more than most in times of recession, when redundancies are plentiful.

Sometimes various areas become synonymous with certain trades — King's Road, Portobello Road, and Carnaby Street, immediately spring to mind, but quite possibly in your own locality there are areas where several second-hand car garages are sited, or a selection of antique shops, or coin dealers, etc. If there is such an area encompassing the types of trade in which you are interested, you will find it beneficial if you open a shop there, and thus take advantage of any existing trade, and even help to bring customers from further afield, by adding even more specialisation to the area.

Each position must be judged by the amount of competition and the number of houses and places of work in the vicinity. Remember, to get a profit you have to have turnover, and you cannot have turnover without people. People mean profit. All to often this is forgotten.

We made this mistake with out first shop. We bought an olde worlde confectionery/tobacconist's business in a delightful high class area, surrounded by large detached houses. The shop was one of 18 covering all trades, but with most duplicated. There was no passing trade and too few houses to support the shops. After a year of gradually getting deeper into debt we decided to cut our losses and managed to sell. We had bought the shop on the recommendation of someone who knew nothing of that type of business, and because it looked pretty, and we fancied living there. We learnt our lesson and checked far more thoroughly in future.

It depends what you are looking for. We were young and needed sufficient income to expand and support our family. This business was useless for us. However, for someone retiring, who wished to enjoy the slow pace of village-type life, was not bothered too much about the level of income, and placed more emphasis on having a friendly chat with the regulars, it was ideal.

Modern Trends

The trend in shopping nowadays is towards fewer trips, made to nearby shops. Parking facilities are very important. Town centre multiple trading and high rents have caused many shop units to become empty, and gradually be taken over by companies not involved in retail trading. To try to combat this, various councils now have a policy of not allowing a change of use from a shop premise in a 'shopping area' to a non-retail use without an adequate shop window display, and sometimes, not even then.

Change of Use

The planning authority needs to be informed only if there is a change of use from one retail trade to another, and this generally presents no problem. If the change of use is to a shop where hot food is sold, the Environmental Health Department will have to be informed, and their consent obtained.

What kind of Shop?

It is best if you decide early on what you expect from a shop, and have a definite objective in mind, rather than just drift into shopkeeping, until it becomes a way of life with you working to keep the shop, rather than the shop keeping you, when it is no longer a viable proposition. Decide why you want a shop. Some reasons are as follows:

(a) You either have been brought up in a business, or have worked in one.
(b) You like the idea of being answerable to no one, and being self-employed.
(c) You like the idea of building up and owning a business, for prestige purposes, or for leaving to your children.
(d) An opportunity has arisen near to where you live, for purchasing an empty shop, and providing a service you feel is lacking in the area.
(e) You may fancy utilising any special knowledge, skill or hobby you have.
(f) You may fancy an easy life (you will soon learn).
(g) Because of ill health it may be the only means of making a living.
(h) Being an eternal optimist, you see it as the only possible means of eventually earning a good living with the minimum of effort.

Having decided why you want a shop, you should next decide on the type of trade to which you are best suited, and then your choice of trading policy. You have to decide on a policy because you cannot cater for all the public and all their different needs, and you must make

your chosen policy known as quickly and widely as possible. You have
to choose between being known for your quality, for your prices, for
your specialised stock, for your service, for your specialised knowledge, for your long hours, for your credit facilities, for your delivery
system, or any combination of these and others. They will all combine
to form an image of your shop in the public eye, and you have to try to
acquire the image you desire. You can test this very simply yourself by
thinking of shops in your locality, and labelling them as being
'exclusive', 'costly', 'friendly', 'knowledgeable', 'stocking top quality',
'in depth selection', etc. Now work it the other way and see which
shops immediately spring to mind, and therefore have the best image,
when you think of 'fruit', 'ham', 'ice cream', 'fillet steak', 'whisky',
'paper clips', 'fresh cream cakes', etc. What makes these shops stand
out from the rest? Study and emulate.

For those of you who have not quite made up your minds, I have
divided shops into the following categories:

(1) SPECIALIST SHOPS: bakers, butchers, chemists, restaurants,
    etc.
(2) SERVICE INDUSTRIES: coin-operated launderettes, dry clean-
    ers, fast photo shops, video shops, etc.
(3) SIMPLE CATERING: Wimpey Bars, Kentucky Fried Chicken,
    basic cafes.
(4) HIGH STOCK VALUES: electrical shops, fancy goods, camera
    shops, toyshops, ironmongers and hardware, jewellers, etc.
(5) DISAPPEARING TRADES: drapers, fishmongers, men's outfit-
    ters, women's clothing.
(6) PUBLIC HOUSES
(7) BREAD AND BUTTER SHOPS (still capable of having jam on):
    delicatessen, grocers, greengrocers, newsagents, post offices.

(1) Specialist Shops

There is no need to dwell on this section, because if you do not have
the required skills, I strongly urge you not to contemplate any of
them. As far as chemists are concerned, it is not necessary to be a
qualified pharmacist to own a chemist, but one must be employed if
you intend to dispense medicines or sell drugs, and a substantial salary
usually has to be offered.

There can be a high degree of wastage in these types of shops, which
if you are not expert could soon turn a theoretically good week's
trading into a mediocre one, and a mediocre one into a loss, despite the
high profit margins. Average gross profit 30 per cent. Restaurants 70
per cent.

(2) Service Industries

These are basically new types of shops, which can be fairly easily learned and run. The most important factor is the position. If you are essentially a gambler it could pay off to take an empty shop in a busy centre and start one from scratch. You could just as easily lose a lot of money because equipment costs are usually high, and High Street shops command top premiums and returns. Personally I would be very wary of buying one of these shops ready trading as they are so easy to set up, and, it seems to me, only sold because they do not reach expectations.

(3) Simple Catering

This falls easily into two types — individually controlled and franchise.

Individually Controlled These can take the form of 'Jack's Transport Cafe' on a main trunk road, a sandwich bar in Oxford Street, a thatched cottage serving fresh cream teas etc. in the countryside, a snack bar in the High Street, a fish and chip shop, or a myriad of other forms including hot dog stands and catering concessions at public places and events. *The advantages* are that you have complete freedom to determine your opening hours, prices, types of food sold, decor, equipment, and all other aspects, providing the Health Regulations are complied with. *The disadvantages* are, if you take over an existing business you will probably not cook in exactly the same manner as your predecessors, and even though your way may be better, some people will be dissatisfied and not come back. If you start a business from scratch it can take quite some time before you build up a reputation and you will have to retain a sufficient amount of money to live on until that time arrives.

Franchises (see also page 33). Wimpy Bars, and most similar fast food ventures, can be bought as going concerns or started from the beginning. Existing shops are advertised and sold in the same manner as other types of business, i.e. privately, and through business transfer agents. New businesses may be started if a suitable site is found which is acceptable to the company concerned. These will only usually be in prime positions in towns with a minimum stated population. All expenses will be paid by you including any premium to get in, installation of equipment, fixtures and fittings, and decorations to a regulation standard. *The advantages* are that you are looked upon as being part of a national company, and the reputation of the company generally, together with all advertising, will allude directly to you. *The disadvantages* are that you have to accept the fact that prices, profit margins, range of foods, buying sources, cleanliness, and the way the business is run and updated, are dictated by the company. More information may be obtained by contacting the companies direct, and they will inform you of their various training schemes. If you are thinking of buying one of these shops in particular, find out if the franchisor has insisted on the franchisee updating the premises or fixtures and fittings.

Generally: There is money to be made in catering, but you have to be prepared to work long hours, probably evening and weekends, and put up with the general public, including rowdy groups, for a much longer period of time than in other types of shop. This does not suit everybody. Gross profit margins are in the region of 55 per cent to 70 per cent.

(4) High Stock Value Shops

These are usually specialist shops carrying a comprehensive range of stock, and are normally found in High Street positions because of the necessity of having a sufficiently large volume of traffic passing the window. Very occasionally this type of shop is found in a secondary or minor location, but this is invariably the result of a long-established business having built up a good reputation in the surrounding area over a number of years, or the result of an extensive advertising programme continually being carried out. No real in-depth knowledge is initially needed for this type of shop, although obviously an interest in the type of product sold is beneficial. The main drawback in buying an existing business is the amount of stock money needed. Generally this money has to be found in full, because banks are not very keen on lending money to buy stock. More of this later. More money is being spent on this type of commodity each year, but as far as the ordinary shop is concerned, this is being offset by large cut-price multiples, and, increasingly, by the growth in popularity of mail order catalogues. Gross profit margins generally range from 25 per cent to 45 per cent.

(5) Disappearing Trades

These have virtually completely disappeared from secondary positions, and are few and far between in the High Streets. The clothing trade has now been almost completely 'sewn up' by department stores, clothing chains, and again, increasingly, mail order catalogues. Gross profit margins in the region of 30 per cent.

(6) Public Houses

Many people dream of buying or retiring to a pub and enjoying the 'good life' for the remainder of their years. They see themselves sitting by the bar or open fire, in a friendly cosy atmosphere, playing 'mine host' to the regulars. They do not realise, or conveniently forget, all the work that has to be done before the bar opens and after it closes. I was brought up in the pub game and know what is involved.

Before the pub can open in the morning the floor has to be swept and washed, the carpets vaccuumed, tables and ashtrays cleaned, chairs brushed off, the bar and pumps washed and polished, bottles of beer brought up from the cellar and stacked on the shelves, the optics checked, the fire cleared out in the winter, fuel brought up from the fuel store and the fire lit, lavatories cleaned out, fresh towels and lavatory paper checked, beer barrels sorted out for the day's trade, the float prepared for the till or tills, and if food is sold, that has also to be prepared. Beer deliveries have to be taken in two or three times a week, sometimes as early as six o'clock in the morning, the cellar has to be washed down regularly, the pipes for draught beer have to be cleaned once a week, empty bottles have to be taken down into the cellar and sorted into appropriate crates, and all the delivery men and draymen have to be checked to make sure they leave the correct number of cases and credit you with the correct number of empties. After the pub closes at night, all the dirty glasses have to be taken in, washed, dried and put away, and the tills checked. This goes on every day and every night, seven days a week, 52 weeks a year. Home life for children is practically non-existent. If this type of life still attracts you, read on, You have two choices.

Tenancies These take several forms, but put simply, means that you buy the fixtures and fittings, pay a relatively small returnable premium to a brewery, plus a yearly rent, together with all the usual outgoings (electricity, gas, rates, telephone, etc.), and are 'tied' to the brewery for purchases of beers, wines and spirits. There are also various types of leases which have almost the same effect. At present there is a dispute as to whether this 'tie' is legal or not. Any profits from the business are yours in exactly the same way as in other trades. Interviews are arranged through specialist brokers. Your first pub is not likely to be very profitable or salubrious, but if you run it properly you can then apply for other better pubs as and when they come up.

Free houses These are what they say — freehold licensed properties which are purchased outright and are free to stock and sell any types of beer and spirits you desire. Because you can choose your own suppliers you are able to buy the same beer cheaper than if you had a tenancy. There are all the normal outgoings, but no rent to pay. Why, you may ask, should anyone buy a tenancy when they can buy a freehold? The answer is very simple. Cash. A free house will cost at least as much as a good four-bedroomed house on a private estate in a pricey area. Details of free houses for sale may be obtained from specialist agents and others in *Dalton's Weekly*. Gross profit margins approximately 45 per cent to 50 per cent (tenancies).

Before leaving the subject of public houses, beware the type of advert that reads something like 'Pub training courses — get practical experience, and then your own pub'. These are usually living-in jobs, very poorly paid, at the end of which you will probably be offered a relief manager's job, shunted here and there for a week at a time, until a suitable pub is available. This whole process will probably take at the very least six months, and all you will be offered at the end will probably be a slum or 'trouble' house. You have been warned.

(7) 'Bread and Butter' Shops

These are the types of shops that have survived in neighourhood parades, and make up the vast bulk of businesses on the market. Carefully chosen, this type of shop provides the best and safest way of going into business and increasing your income. There now follows a brief description of each type of shop, together with main advantages and disadvantages. Some general stores may be comprised of many of the following sections.

Grocers With the advent of the modern supermarket many small grocers have been forced to close through lack of support from local residents who prefer to spend the money they save on a few groceries, on bus fares and petrol travelling to the nearest town centre, so that they may then compare the prices between different multiples. The picture in the last couple of years has changed however, as the multiples themselves have found that their smaller supermarkets are no longer profitable, and have closed them down. The trend now is to close several larger supermarkets in an area, and open a superstore or hypermarket instead, which will draw custom from a much larger area. The cost of running a superstore of say 100,000 sq ft out of town, is far less than the cost of running ten 10,000 sq ft units in prime positions. This is all good news for the grocer, and ensures a long future as long as he is not next to a proposed hypermarket. Sales of fresh food continue to increase. Frozen food accounts for approximately 8 per cent of all grocery sales in the UK, but there are conflicting views as to whether the market is expanding or declining. In 1984 the average sales per shop assistant should have been about £850 per week, and total turnover should have been in the region of £4 per sq ft of selling area. *The advantages* are easy hours, Bank Holidays if you wish, cheap food for yourself, and once properly organised, no need to do anything after you close in the evening. *The disadvantages* are possible confrontations with over-zealous Health Officers, and having to listen to the same old customers moaning they can buy a tin of beans twopence cheaper down the road. Gross profit should be 15 per cent to 20 per cent.

Greengrocers Profit margins are determined by whether or not you go to market yourself, or have the goods delivered. *The advantages* are easy hours, Bank Holidays. *The disadvantages* are the early mornings, if produce is bought from market, and hot weather can play havoc with stock and wastage levels. Gross profit approximately 25 per cent.

Delicatessens These need a better trading position than an ordinary grocer, and a more specialised knowledge, which is not too hard to acquire. *The advantages* are similar to grocers, as are *the disadvantages*, apart from the fact that prices are definitely secondary to quality. Gross profit approximately 30 per cent.

Post Offices Post Office salaries are determined by the amount of work carried out at the office. Every type of transaction carries its own unit value, determined by the length of time the average transaction takes. These units are added together and the total is then matched to the appropriate scale salary. Salaries are reviewed every three years (triennial revisions), and may go down as well as up. Each year a pay increase is negotiated by the Subpostmasters Federation, which is usually paid about October, and back-dated to April. You can ask for a special revision if you feel your trade has increased substantially since the last triennial.

The advantages are very easy hours, and the knowledge that you will receive 'x' amount of pounds at the end of the month, regardless of how busy or quiet you have been. You also have all the Bank Holidays.

The disadvantages. Because of their regular guaranteed income, post offices are more expensive to buy than other shops showing the same gross profit. There is a danger of injury through hold-ups, and also a threat at the moment of closing a number of offices regardless of their size or salary. What is just as worrying for subpostmasters, is the tendency for the post office to try and reduce the number of units by trying to persuade the public to have their family allowances paid monthly, and pensions paid direct into a bank. The family allowance and pension work is a substantial part of most offices' salaries, and all cuts will be felt by the subpostmasters' pockets. Family allowances which are paid weekly, mean four dockets per month; at say one unit per docket, this equals four units per month. When family allowances are paid monthly, their value is one unit only. It does not matter that you are paying out the same amount of money, it is the dockets that count. In the case of pensions, if they are paid through the bank there is a loss of four units per month also. It must be said that the post office is introducing new business into suboffices all the time, such as Datapost, travellers' cheques, flowers by post, Transcash, stationery, etc., but these generate hardly any business at all, and do not even scratch the surface of units lost elsewhere. Loans at preferential rates are available to subpostmasters for improving their shops and fittings generally.

If you are about to purchase a sub-post office, you must make sure the sale can be nullified in the event of you not being appointed subpostmaster. This is achieved by having a clause inserted in the contract stating that after exchange of contracts the vendor will tender his resignation and you will apply for the post, but if you are not appointed within, say, 14 weeks of exchange of contracts, the sale will be null and void. Alternatively, the sale could still proceed, but at a reduced price, if the terms for this are previously agreed.

In actual fact, the appointment of a subpostmaster has nothing to do with the actual business. The existing postmaster must first tender his resignation, (three months notice is required), and then the vacant post is advertised for three weeks in neighbouring post offices, during which time anyone may apply. This ritual is governed by regulations and has to be adhered to. Interviews are held, characters are assessed, and proposed locations considered. However, as alternative sites have the disadvantages of having to obtain planning permission, possible delays in alterations to premises for easy access and security, and general inconvenience to the public in moving the location, it is very unusual for the purchaser of the business to be unsuccessful in his application. In order to be appointed subpostmaster or subpostmistress, the regional head postmaster has to find you acceptable and of 'good character'. Two or three weeks training is given in a suitable post office, during which time you will be paid a wage, and as already stated, three months notice of termination will be required from either side.

Liquor Licences These licences are held by individuals, not by shops or public houses, and must be applied for personally. Applications are submitted to the local Licensing Justices, at which time the Police will have a chance to object to the granting of the licence after investigating your character and past history. When purchasing one of these businesses, it is necessary to have a clause inserted in the contract covering the possibility of the licence not being granted.

Newsagents As far as newsagents are concerned, the newspaper side, because of its very nature, has remained a protected species. It is very difficult for other shops in the vicinity to be supplied with newspapers, although wholesalers deny there is a closed shop. Other sections of the news/confectionery/tobacconist trade have been hit to a degree by cut-pricing on cigarettes and confectionery, especially Christmas boxes of chocolates and Easter eggs, but as the majority of confectionery sales are impulse buys, trade generally has not altered too much. *The advantages.* Newspapers carry a good profit margin. A healthy wholesale news bill, especially through morning deliveries, will ensure a steady trade and a decent overall gross profit. *The disadvantages* are early mornings every day of the week; occasional trouble with paper boys, ending up with you having to go out and deliver the papers yourself (usually in the pouring rain); Sunday opening; and because of the health aspect, a poor future for the cigarette industry. Gross profit 15 per cent to 20 per cent depending on the wholesale newsbill and the extent to which the price of cigarettes is cut.

Will it be Profitable?

Approximate gross profit margins have been given after each section as a guide for reference purposes only, and for comparing with the gross profit shown on the actual accounts of the shop you are interested in. It is not a guide to the profitability of a shop. This is determined by many factors which we shall go into in more detail later in the book. Suffice it to say at the moment that a grocer taking £3,000 per week at 15 per cent gross profit will earn £450 per week *gross*, and a fancy goods shop with a trade of £2,000 per week at 35 per cent gross profit will earn £700 per week *gross*. Gross profit is therefore determined by multiplying the takings by the expected gross profit percentage margin.

Try to get some experience of the trade you fancy before actually committing yourself and your money. This can be done by the husband or wife obtaining a full-time or part-time job in a similar business locally. Full-time is obviously better, but even this will not give a full insight into what is actually involved in running a business, although it will certainly show you what it is like to deal with the general public. By far the best method is to go on a week's comprehensive training course in the preferred trade.

How to Find a Business

Now you've decided what kind of business you want — how do you find it?

(1) The most obvious and common method is to study the advertisements placed by business transfer agents in specialist papers such as *Dalton's Weekly*. These give brief details of many businesses, and invite you to contact the agents for further details. Contact as many agents as possible who cover the area you are looking at. When you read the shop descriptions bear in mind that the agent works for, and gets his commission from, the vendor. You can be sure that he will advertise *ALL* the good points, and in some cases, a few points that are not even there. You will notice that he is covered against these 'oversights' by a disclaimer somewhere on the details stating something like 'Although these descriptions and dimensions are believed to

be accurate, this is not guaranteed, we are not responsible for any loss arising thereof, and they do not form any part of a contract'. It will be up to you to find the *BAD* points. Most businesses you will find, seem to bear no relationship to their dazzling descriptions. Many a time we have driven literally hundreds of miles to look at a shop that appeared to be absolutely perfect on paper, only to find that a new supermarket was about to be opened, or had just been opened, almost next door, or that a new superstore or hypermarket was about to be built a mile away. Once, we drove from Worthing to a small village in Devon to see a pub that had the most glowing reports. When we arrived, we found it was situated by itself surrounded by fields, and completely empty.

(2) Another method is by replying to private advertisements. These are usually placed with a box number, and are usually either businesses that have just been placed on the market and are trying to be sold without having to pay agents' fees, or shops that have been hanging around for some time and the owners are getting desperate. Reply to these by all means, but do not be surprised if you do not get an answer.

(3) You can place a wanted advertisement in *Dalton's Weekly*, or the trade paper or magazine.

(4) You can contact wholesalers, representatives etc., and ask them if they know of any businesses for sale, and to keep an eye open for you. They will sometimes know of a business before it actually goes on the market, and will usually be very helpful if they believe you will continue to trade with them.

(5) If you are looking for a business in a particular area, type out a letter stating that you are looking for a suitable business in that area, and asking the owner to telephone you if he is thinking of selling now or in the near future. Have these photocopied, address them to 'The Owner', marking the envelope 'Personal — Private and Confidential', and drop them through the letter box of any shop you like the look of. If you are not in a hurry to find a business, this could be your best bet. Follow the letter up every few months with a reminder.

Looking over the Shop

Having made a short list of viable-looking businesses, it is now time to look them over. From the details already provided by the agent or owner, you will know the weekly turnover, how long the lease has to go (if leasehold), when the rent reviews are, how much the rent is, what the gross profit or percentage is, and you will also have a brief description of the accommodation, if applicable. You may also have been informed that true net profits are excellent, and that 'working owners could expect to earn £ . . . pa'. You will know the type of location of the shop, and may even be told the reason the vendor wishes to sell. Some of the most common reasons are given below, with my comments underneath.

Why does he want to sell?

Other business interests In other words, he does not think there is enough profit in that shop, and no future worth considering.

Giving up because of ill health Either this has been brought about by him having to work 24 hours a day, seven days a week, because he cannot afford to employ staff, or the continual worry of impending doom is turning him grey.

Emigrating After 'x' number of years in the shop, he wants to run away as far as possible.

Buying a larger business There is not enough to be made from the present one

Due to family problems He can see a dwindling income for his family.

It is very useful to find out the real reason for selling, but as you can see from the comments above, I take the ones actually given, with a pinch of salt. It is best to completely disregard the vendor's reasons, and try to find out for yourself. This may be harder than you think, because the vendor has been in touch with all the local gossip and trends for a long time, and has had plenty of opportunity to present the business in the best possible light. After all, you are not inspecting the business at your leisure, but when he wants you to. Even if the explanation checks out, you may still not have found the real reason.

As an example, there was the case of the vendor who stated that he had tendered for a shop several months ago, which was due to be built by a local authority on the south coast. The shop was to have a monopoly position, and had excellent prospects. His tender was successful, but as the shop was a considerable distance away, he had decided to sell his present one and move down there. Anyone checking this reason would have verified it in every respect. Surely this was a genuine sale? However, delving deeper it transpired that one of the reasons he had put in an offer for the development in the first place, was the fact that he had heard there was to be a new parade of shops going to be built near his own, and he wanted to get out before his trade suffered. And who can blame him? Wouldn't you do the same if there was a risk of losing most of your investment, being forced to sell up, and finding yourself and your family out on the streets? I know I would. Remember, the vendor's first priority is to himself, his wife, and his children. Incidentally, the real reason for the aforesaid sale could have been discovered if the vendor's bank manager had been approached for a substantial loan.

Buying and selling a business is rather like a game of chess. When you are buying, you have the disadvantage of joining the game after the vendor has played all the moves he wants, and then trying to discover how and why he is in his current position. The real reason may be the one he states, but you would be well advised to look elsewhere first.

A Selection of REAL *reasons to check on*

Competition This can be in the form of a proposed new shopping development in the vicinity, which, it is feared, will erode trade. This may be discovered by a slow drive round all the streets in the catchment area, a look in the local papers, or a friendly chat in the local pub. Competition may also be coming from a shop on the same parade, which is trying to muscle in on his trade. This also is quite easily checked on by a walk round all the other nearby shops. Another reason may be that he has heard that a nearby empty shop will be opened in competition. Look at any empty shops, and telephone the agent whose name appears outside on the board, to try and get as much information as possible about its proposed use. Yet another form of competition may be coming from a shop in a different trade, who has applied for a change of use. This may be checked from the planning officer of the local authority. Generally, speak to as many people as possible, including local shop assistants. Do not be afraid to mention that the shop is for sale. After all, it is your money you are trying to protect. In any case, it will not make any difference to the vendor, because his customers will not stop using his shop, and any assistants, if they are not already aware of the position, soon will be.

Development Another reason for selling could be the threat of development. This might take the form of compulsory purchase by the local council for a new development or road widening. This can be checked by a visit or telephone call to the local authority. It will be checked as a matter of course by your solicitor at a later date anyway, if you agree to purchase.

Rent increase This may have already happened at a rent review, and made the business far less viable in the eyes of the vendor, although perhaps not so to a purchaser. This is very easy to understand, because everyone gets used to a certain level of income, and becomes dissatisfied when this is decreased due to a rent increase. It happens to us all. On the other hand it may be that a rent renewal or review is coming up, and the vendor has an intimation of what the new rent is likely to be, and considers that when that happens he will not be able to make a reasonable living.

Bad buy If the vendor has not been in the shop for very long, it is possible that he bought it assuming the takings were a set figure, without verification, and now finding they are not, wants to get out and get his money back. If there are no accounts to hand, determine exactly when he bought the business. Be suspicious anyway of anyone who has only been in the shop for a short time, and in these circumstances do not take too much notice of the accounts.

A fall in the takings With the acceptance of inflation nowadays, any shop that does not actually increase annual sales, has a declining trade. You have to increase your sales value in relation to inflation, in order to stand still. Any shop that is actually taking less money than that shown for the previous year, is not in a very healthy position, unless it can be proved that the sales mix has been altered to show a higher gross profit, or perhaps, expenses have been cut, such as staff wages. If the takings have dropped, some possible causes are:

(a) Another shop has started trading, and because it is cheaper/larger, etc. it has drawn some of the custom.
(b) A key shop on the parade has closed e.g. a post office, and the public is now using another parade.
(c) A local factory or office block has moved to new premises elsewhere or perhaps has closed down.
(d) It is a dying type of trade.
(e) The country is in a recession, and all types of trade are suffering.
(f) A new bus route has been introduced elsewhere, or the existing one cut out, or re-routed.
(g) Yellow lines have been painted outside.
(h) Loss of enthusiasm on the part of the owner.
(i) Because of possible financial pressure, the stock value has been reduced, and the shop is now understocked.

When selecting a shop, bear in mind that regardless of how you feel at the moment, you may wish to sell it again in the not too distant future, and you should not therefore buy a shop which has only limited appeal, unless you can do so at a very keen price. In other words, do not pay over the odds for something which appeals to you, and on which you will lose money if you have to sell quickly.

The shop itself

As far as the actual shop is concerned, pay particular attention to the following:

Parking To realise the full potential of a shop there should be adequate car parking facilities either directly outside, or within easy walking distance. This caters for the car owner who will willingly travel twice as far if he can park easily. It is also important if the goods you sell are bulky.

Inside and outside Take a good look at the outside of the shop. Is there any immediate expense involved? Would more people be encouraged to use it if it were altered in some fashion? Inside the shop, look at the floor covering. Study the condition of any equipment, fixtures and fittings, and make a mental note of any items that look as if they need replacing.

Range of goods Is the range of goods sufficient? Could any ancilliary lines be added to advantage? Is the stock well displayed, and does it look 'fresh'?

The 'price image' Look at the prices of the most popular items to get a 'price image' of the shop.

Attitudes of staff Try to go into the shop when it is open, purely as a customer, and see if you would be encouraged to return. Take note of the assistants' eagerness to serve, their appearance and efficiency.

Extending the sales area Is there any possibility of extending the sales area, either by knocking down a wall between the shop and a stockroom, or by building on at the back or side?

Accommodation Could you live in the accommodation?

Flat Roofs These are a curse. You can reckon on having to renew them every ten years. Bear the cost of repairs in mind.

The future of the parade What do the other shops on the parade look like? How does it compare with other parades nearby? Is any development happening on a nearby parade that might entice customers generally to shop there in future?

The bottom line Do you think customers will carry on using the parade? Could the trade be increased by smartening up the shop, improving the stock, extending the sales area, or changing the attitudes of the present staff? How much expenditure is needed to replace equipment?

PART 2

The Money Side

What Can You Afford?

Buying a business is rather like buying a house, but more complicated. If you were looking for a house you would have to find out how much cash you would have left after selling any assets you might want to dispose of, deducting a sum for any agents' fees, solicitors, stamp duty, removals, etc., and then deciding whether to buy a house outright with your capital, or whether to use this capital as a deposit, and then buy a more expensive house with the aid of a mortgage. Most people, in actual fact, do not have this option, and *have* to choose the latter course. You would then contact several building societies to see how much of a mortgage they would advance, and this figure added to your capital would be your limit. It would be a complete waste of time looking at houses far in excess of this price. On the other hand you would not be doing yourself justice if you looked far below it. You will find, even in the price bracket you have decided upon, many, many shops that look absolutely ideal on paper, and prove useless for one reason or another eventually, when you rush off to view them. You will learn that what is *not* written in the glowing description of a shop is just as important as what *is* written.

Your first job then, is to find out how much capital you will have if you sold your house, paid off any mortgage, and settled solicitors' costs plus estate agents' fees if appropriate, and any other incidentals. Add to this any savings you may wish to put into the business and you now have your total capital to invest.

Your next decision depends to an extent on this figure. You have to decide whether you want a freehold or a leasehold business, and whether to take a loan or not. If you have not been in business before and own your house, your immediate reaction will probably be something like 'I would only buy a freehold, possibly with the aid of a mortgage'. We shall look first of all then at freehold shops, and see what you can afford.

Freehold

Without a loan your maximum price will be your capital less solicitors' fees, etc., less the cost of the stock in trade. As an example, if you have capital of £100,000 and wanted to buy a high stock value shop, it might come out something like this: Solicitors' Charges etc. £3,000 + stock £25,000 = purchase price £72,000. With the same capital if you were looking at a 'Bread and Butter Shop' it might look something like: Solicitors' charges etc. £3,000 + stock £9,000 = purchase price £88,000 approximately.

To work it the other way round, simply add the value of the stock in trade to the solicitors' charges etc., and add this to the asking price. For example, to be able to afford a grocer's shop costing £70,000, you would need stock plus solicitor's charges, perhaps £10,000, which would make a total cost of £80,000.

With a loan your total costings are still worked out as above, but you will have to convince your bank that there will be sufficient profit in the business to be able to repay them in a reasonable time. A reasonable time for banks is ten to twelve years. You can forget about building societies for business purchases apart from special circumstances or when there is a glut of mortgages around. Have a chat with your bank manager, tell him what you have in mind, see if he agrees in principle to a loan, and find out how much the repayments will be per £1,000 over different periods of years. If, after doing all your sums, you find you cannot afford the type of business you desired, do not despair. Start looking at leasehold properties. You will certainly not be in the minority. Most shops are leasehold, including the majority of the big names in the High Streets, with the exception of a few of the very old-established stores.

Leasehold

Your costings are worked out as above except that you will have to retain sufficient cash also to pay for three months rent in advance. Bank loans may be obtained for up to approximately 50 per cent of the purchase price, excluding stock, and will probably have to be repaid over three to five years. Again it will be helpful if you discuss this with your bank manager, and obtain approximate repayment figures per £1,000 over different periods of time.

Having now decided how much you can afford to pay, start looking at businesses which are slightly more expensive. Most prices are set over-optimistically, and unless buyers are falling over themselves to pay a deposit, you can assume a fairly close offer will be accepted.

This just leaves the question of whether it is best to buy with a loan or not. Perhaps the best way of illustrating this is by giving some examples. These are not meant as unshakeable rules and regulations, but are given so that you will be able to understand the whole situation more fully, and not ignore opportunities that may arise because of preconceived ideas.

Examples
(These are of course hypothetical cases)

SHOP A
Takings £1,000 per week @ 18 per cent GP. Rent £1,500 p.a.
Gross Profit £9,360 p.a. Expenses — staff, rent, etc. £4,000 p.a.
Price £15,000 *leasehold or Freehold £50,000.* Stock £2,500.
Net Profit leasehold after paying all expenses including rent — £5,360 p.a.

SHOP B
Takings £2,000 per week @ 18 per cent GP. Rent £2,400 p.a.
Gross Profit £18,720 p.a. Expenses — staff, rent, etc., £9,700 p.a.
Price £23,000 *Leasehold or Freehold £65,000.* Stock £4,500.
Net Profit Leasehold After Paying All Expenses Including rent — £9,000 p.a.

SHOP C
Takings £3,000 per week @ 18 per cent GP. Rent £2,500 p.a.
Gross Profit £28,000 p.a. Expenses — staff, rent, etc., £20,000 p.a.
Price £32,000 *Leasehold or Freehold £75,000.* Stock £6,500.
Net Profit leasehold after paying all expenses including rent — £13,300 p.a.

SHOP D
Takings £4,000 per week @ 18 per cent GP. Rent £3,000 p.a.
Gross Profit £37,440 p.a. Expenses — Staff, rent, etc. £20,000 p.a.
Price £42,000 *Leasehold or Freehold £90,000.* Stock £9,000.
Net Profit leasehold after paying all expenses including rent — £17,900 p.a.

After putting aside £5,000 for legal fees and a bit in the bank, three typical purchasers' finances might look like this:

Mr 'X' has £18,000 capital. Mr 'Y' has £28,000, and Mr 'Z' has £40,000.

Each has the choice of buying outright or with a loan. Let us look at the various choices open to them.

Mr 'X'
Could buy SHOP A leasehold outright and have left £5,360
He would not earn sufficient to repay a mortgage, and cannot buy the F/H. He could buy SHOP B with a loan of £10,000 (repayments £3,500 p.a.) and have £5,500 p.a.

Mr 'Y'
Could buy SHOP B outright leasehold and have left .... £9,000p.a.
He could buy SHOP C (loan £10,500 repayments £3,700 p.a.) and have £10,400p.a.
He also does not have sufficient money to even buy SHOP A freehold.

Mr 'Z'

Could buy SHOP C outright leasehold and have left ...... £13,300p.a.
Could buy SHOP D (loan £11,000 repayments £3,800 p.a.) and have
£14,100p.a.
Could buy SHOP A with a £12,500 mortgage and be left with
£3,500p.a.

What does all the above prove? You could say I have rigged all the
figures to give a biased viewpoint, but you must agree, on the face of
it, it is much better buying a shop with a loan, apart from it being a
form of saving, after it has been repaid the repayment figures become
extra profit, and of course your business is worth much more. Every
proposition will have to be judged on its own merits, but there is a
very good case for moving every five years, once a loan has been
repaid. As a final example using the above fictitious shops, let us take
the case of a man who has £100,000 to invest, and see what options are
open to him . . .

He could buy:

SHOP D outright, live over the shop, and earn .... £20,900p.a.
SHOP D leasehold outright, a house for £50,000 outright and earn
.... £17,900p.a.

A shop taking more money leasehold outright and earn in excess of
£28,000 p.a. or any number of other combinations.

All of the above examples are intended to make you consider the
various options open to you very carefully. There is one last thought I
will leave you with whilst on this subject. Many people would rather
buy a freehold shop than a leasehold, knowing that they will earn less
money initially, but thinking that when they have paid off the
mortgage, they will be better off. Is this true? Generally, no one will
argue that if you repay a loan of, say £20,000, on a freehold property,
and a loan of the same amount against a leasehold business, you will
earn more from the leasehold during the duration of the loan, than
from the freehold. The real question then, must be, what do you
intend doing after the loan is repaid? If your object is to stay there for
the rest of your life, content with your income, free from rent reviews
and renewals, and surveyors' inspections, then fine, that is your path.
But what if you intend moving on to something better? The value of
the business will be the same, freehold or leasehold, and you will now
be faced with exactly the same problem you had originally, i.e. to buy
freehold or leasehold. The big difference though, is that you will have
earned more per annum during the period of the loan, from the
leasehold shop.

Do not take all the above as definite rules. Each shop must be
judged individually, and it would be foolhardy not to take advantage
of a freehold if it were offered at a bargain price.

A Real-Life Example

It is worth a quick look at a genuine case concerning a very good friend of mine who was going into business for the first time, and was not keen on the thought of buying a leasehold business. He sold his house, realised some other assets, and had a total capital of £23,000 to invest in a shop, after paying for stock and other expenses. He found a freehold grocer's taking £3,200 per week, and the asking price was £62,000. The woman who owned the shop had matrimonial problems, and was desperate to sell. He managed to buy the business for £55,000 with the aid of a £32,000 mortgage from the bank, repayable at £6,200 p.a. On the face of it he had a very good buy — a £3,200 per week shop for £55,000 freehold. Let us see what else he could have done with his £23,000 instead.

For this exercise we shall ignore inflation, and assume that a figure of 8 per cent of the weekly turnover will cover all expenses apart from rent and repayments. If he had managed to make an equally good buy, and ended up with a leasehold shop taking £5,000 per week, for £46,000 (50 per cent loan), we would have the following comparison chart:

Takings	GP @ 15 per cent	8 per cent Expenses	Mortgage/ loan	Rent	Net Profit
£3,200	£24,960	£13,312	£6,240	—	£7,072
£5,000	£39,000	£20,800	£7,130	£5,000	£8,670

Therefore for the first five years he would have had £1,600 per annum extra in his pocket. It would have been more actually, because the entire amount of the rent would have gone against tax relief, whereas with a mortgage only the interest qualifies. Incidentally, the above mortgage loan figures are based on a ten-year period for the mortgage, and a five-year period for the loan.

If he then sold the leasehold business after five years for the same amount he paid for it (£46,000 — remember we are ignoring inflation), he could buy another for £75,000, and perhaps have the following comparison for the next five years:

Takings	GP @ 15 per cent	8 per cent Expenses	Mortgage/ loan	Rent	Net Profit
£3,200	£24,960	£13,312	£6,240	—	£7,072
£8,000	£62,400	£33,280	£9,000	£8,000	£16,280

Therefore after ten years in the freehold shop, he has earned a total of £70,720, and has a property worth say, £60,000. After completing the above leasehold exercise, he has a business worth £75,000, and has earned a total of £124,750. You might now say 'OK, but with the freehold business he now has no mortgage to pay, which will increase his earnings to £13,312, whereas regardless of takings, the rent of the leasehold shop will rise again and make that a worse proposition!' Ignoring the fact that we have ignored inflation, and therefore the rent should not rise, the crux of the matter is, what would the position be if each shop were sold after ten years? On the above figures the leasehold wins hands down. It has provided £54,000 more income, and is worth £15,000 more.

The answer then, must be, if you want to make money buy leasehold and keep moving to larger businesses with the aid of loans. If, on the other hand, you desire a business where you could quite contentedly spend the rest of your life, and are satisfied with the income, buy freehold.

There is yet another aspect of the freehold/leasehold question that should be looked into if at all possible, and that is where the shop is being sold leasehold, but the vendor also owns the freehold. In these circumstances it may be possible to purchase the freehold, and find that the mortgage repayments are not much more than the amount asked for the rent. This happened to us several years ago. We were buying a post office confectionery/tobacconist business that had been on the market for some time, and from which the owner wished to retire through ill health. After lengthy negotiations, he eventually agreed to sell the freehold to us, and gave us a 100 per cent loan for this purpose, over ten years at a fixed rate of interest. We found that our mortgage repayments worked out to approximately £150 more per year than the original rent asked. Incidentally, we were also taking a full loan on the goodwill part of the business from our bank.

Finding the Money

Having worked out how much money is needed to complete your purchase, your next step is to arrange the finance. This could come from any of the following sources:

(1) Relations

These have the advantages of not requiring references, giving quick decisions, and possibly not insisting on exorbitant interest rates. Possible disadvantages are that they may want to consistently give 'advice' on the running of the business, and could leave you in an embarrassing situation if they suddenly find they need to have the money repaid. A reasonable rate of interest should be offered, and it is as well to have some form of written agreement stating how you intend repaying the money, and over what period.

(2) Friends

Any borrowing from friends should be done on a more official basis, giving full details of purchase price, how much you intend to invest of your own money, and what sort of return you expect. They should receive interest on their investment, and may wish to have some form of security from you. Again a written agreement setting out the repayment terms is advisable.

(3) Insurance Policies

If you have any Life Insurance Policies that have been in existence for several years, and have a repayment value on maturity, it would probably be well worth while not to cash them in, but to find out the maximum loans that the insurance companies will offer against them. These have two advantages over bank loans. Firstly, they are generally cheaper, and secondly, you have the choice of repaying only the interest if you wish, and leaving the capital to a later date. In fact you may not repay any of the capital at all, in which case the outstanding amount will be deducted from the final figure due to you on maturity. There are no formalities, interviews, or references to provide, because in effect you are borrowing your own money, and the whole thing can generally be arranged fairly quickly.

(4) Commercial Banks

Regardless of what anyone tells you, banks provide the cheapest form of loan, apart from the three sources mentioned above.

Always telephone for an appointment to see your bank manager, and do not arrive late for the interview. Take with you as many details of the business as you can, including an agent's description, copies of the last three years' accounts if possible, and a sheet of paper on which you will have written legibly, or preferably typed, a complete breakdown of your proposed expenses, anticipated income and gross profit, and the amount you should be able comfortably to repay per annum.

Do not be too dejected if your request is turned down by your own bank. This may be due to Bank of England restrictions, or the policy of your bank at the present time, or may even be agreed by your local branch manager, and then turned down by his head office.

Many people advise sticking to the same bank regardless, saying that you will build up a special relationship with them over the years. I have not found this to be so, especially nowadays when virtually every move made by a bank manager is watched over by a computer. In actual fact, what happens in practice, is that if you can prove that the business you require the loan for is profitable, and is capable of repaying the loan over say, five or six years, and you are able to offer sufficient security against the loan, the odds are that you will get it. If you cannot fulfil all three requirements, it is doubtful. The 'special relationship' built up with your bank over the years is nothing more than their knowledge that the longer you stay in business successfully, the more collateral you will have, and the safer will be their money. Successful businessmen may delude themselves about their special relationship, but ask any businessman who had an account at the same bank for the same length of time, and who is scraping the barrel and needs an unsecured loan, what he thinks, and you will get a totally different answer.

Anyway, if the answer is 'No', shop around. Ask your solicitor, or accountant, or successful business friend if they can introduce you to their bank manager. If this is not possible, try different banks yourself to see their reaction. The vendor's bank will provide an interesting answer. This line of enquiry is worth following anyway, because who is in a better position to comment on the financial standing of the business in question? Not that the bank will divulge the state of the vendor's bank balances to you, but if he refuses a largish loan, knowing the general trend of the business and surrounding area, and any likelihood of the appearance of any adverse opposition, beware. Banks do not like to lose customers, but they like losing money even less. As far as repayment terms are concerned, they generally like leaseholds to be repaid over about five years, and freeholds over ten to fifteen years.

(5) Merchant Banks

If the amount of the loan is not acceptable to a commercial bank and you are still determined to go ahead with the purchase, you can try the merchant banks either direct, or if you are buying through an agent, on their introduction. Repayment rates will be higher, regardless of how the interest rates are described. I could write pages on different methods of expressing interest rates, and how to convert one to another, but this is confusing and unnecessary. There is a very simple method of comparing. Obtain actual repayment figures over set numbers of years from different sources, find out if they are fixed or if they will alter with changes in the Bank Rate, then compare, and decide. Of course, if your only means of finance is through a merchant bank, your only choice is whether to buy the shop or not.

If you borrow money, from whatever source, your prime objective should be to repay it as soon as possible, thus starting yourself off on a 'special relationship' basis, and making any future borrowing much easier. To achieve this, it may be necessary initially to cut down on, or do without holidays, and generally draw in your horns with regard to personal spending.

When determining how much you need, do not forget that apart from the actual cost of the business, you will have to pay for your solicitor, surveyor (if one is used), stocktaker, and Stamp Duty. Stamp Duty is payable on both freehold and leasehold properties over £30,000. Fixtures and fittings and stock do not count for Stamp Duty.

(6) Leasebacks

This is a means of raising capital at any time if you are purchasing or own a freehold shop. It entails selling the freehold part of the business to either an investment company or a private investor, and taking a lease in return. You negotiate in the normal manner on the freehold price paid, against the length of lease you require, together with revision periods, and amount of rent offered. It may mean that you will now be able to afford a business that is being sold freehold, or it may raise sufficient capital at a later date to either get you out of trouble, or raise some finance for further expansion.

Before You Buy . . . Valuing the Business

To state the obvious, the price quoted on the details of the business from the agents will be something like '£20,000 s.a.v.'. This means that the price required for the shop, including the lease, goodwill, and fixtures and fittings is £20,000, and that added to that figure will be a sum of money for the stock, which will be valued on the day of completion.

Volumes have been written about how to value a business. They include multiplying the 'adjusted' net profit by any fraction between one and three, plus the result of working out a straight line method of depreciation for fixtures and fittings, plus a value for the lease which is determined by one of various ways, and a myriad of other mystical methods.

In practice, buying a shop is like buying a house. You look at as many as possible which have the features you desire, and then choose the one that gives the most for the least money. In other words, you choose the one that suits you and is the best value. It is immaterial what price you arrive at after doing the most complicated sums, if you cannot find a vendor to accept your figures.

All I can suggest, as far as making an offer is concerned, is to decide how much you are prepared to pay, and offer a couple of thousand less, and do not be in a rush.

Potential

If the potential for the shop is obvious, such as a new housing estate in the process of being built around a newagent's or grocer's, with no other new shops planned, it is worth paying more for the business. If the potential is not as obvious as this, but still there, it may be worthwhile paying a small extra premium. What you should ask yourself constantly, is that if the potential is so good, why is the vendor selling now, and not waiting until the trade improves and then obtaining a much higher figure for the shop? If the potential is for opening longer hours, it should be ignored, because any improvement in the trade from this area will have come about from your own efforts, and it is you who should reap the benefit from them.

Christmas Clubs

Enquiries should be made as to whether there is a Christmas Club in existence. Many shops run these clubs, whereby customers deposit sums of money with the shopkeeper, not necessarily on a regular basis, and then use the credit built up during the year to obtain the goods of their choice at Christmas. Depending on how hard the Christmas Club has been promoted in the shop, will depend the amount of cash involved, but if it is an active club and late in the year, a considerable sum of money could be involved. All transactions should have been recorded in a Christmas Club Book, and this should be totalled on the day of completion, and the cash handed over to the purchaser, or the total added to the stock value.

If such a club is not discovered until a later date, it could prove both costly and embarrassing if there is any difficulty in obtaining the cash from the vendor. In this case you would have the choice of bearing the cost yourself, or risk losing a large number of regular customers by refusing to pay them, on the grounds that any money given to the vendor is of no concern or responsibility of yours. (More about Christmas Clubs on page 117.)

Surveys

If the shop you are about to purchase is freehold, you will obviously have a survey carried out, if not for your own peace of mind, certainly for that of the mortgagor. But what about leasehold? As the majority of leases nowadays are 'fully repairing and insuring', it is as well to find out the worst beforehand, and at least be prepared. In any case, as with house surveys, if anything of any consequence shows up, it is usually possible to get a reduction of the price at least equal to that of the cost of the survey. Bear in mind also, that it may come in handy one day to have an official report on the condition of the premises when you took over.

Do-it-yourself market surveys

Have you ever thought of commissioning a specialist firm to do a market survey on a particular shop in order to find out what the actual

Good Morning/Afternoon, Madam

We are carrying out a shopping survey for the Food Trades, in the Westchester area, and wondered if you would mind helping us by answering a few questions?

(1) Do you tend to shop Daily (a), Main shopping once a week plus odd items during the week (b).

(2) At which store do you do the bulk of your shopping?

(3) Why? Cheap prices (a), Friendly (b), Clean (c), Selection (d), Parking (e).

(4) How much do you spend there on average?

(5) Do you use any of the local shops? If so, which?

(6) How much do you spend on average per week in your local food shop?

(7) What image would you say the shop has — Friendly (a), Expensive (b), Cheap (c), Clean (d), Dirty (e)?

(8) What do you think of the special offers? Too dear (a), not enough (b), don't know (c)?

(9) What type of goods do you normally buy there? Confectionery (a), Meat (b), Greengrocery (c), Cigarettes (d), Grocery (e), Frozen (f).

(10) Which would you never buy there?

(11) Why?

(12) How do you think it could be improved?

(13) If it were, do you think you would use it more?

(14) Where do you buy your greengrocery? Supermarket (a), greengrocer (b), Farm Shop (c), local food shop (d), market (e).

(15) Do you have newspapers delivered?

(16) Where do you buy your golf balls?

(17) How often do your play?

(18) Where?

(19) Do you lose many balls?

(20) What do you think of strawberry-flavoured ones?

customers think of it? If you are looking at several shops, this would obviously be a very expensive exercise. However, you can do the same thing for yourself at the cost of a few hours only, and if you have asked the right questions, either end up with a definite plan of action, or forget the site altogether.

Here is how you go about it. Obtain a street plan of the immediate area, and mark all the shops within a half-mile radius. From this you should be able to see the catchment area, which may be a mid-distance from the next opposition, or may be determined by other factors such as playing fields, a large factory, a private estate, a river, or even a steep hill. What you have to discover is, are the people who live very local to the shop using it, and if not, why not? Where are the boundary line customers shopping? If the answer is 'at the opposition', why do they prefer it?

I have made out a sample questionnaire for the grocery trade which is shown on the previous page and a suggestion for recording the answers shown below. You can think up your own questions relating to your own trade, and if you are thinking of starting something new, such as selling strawberry-flavoured golf balls, you can even get their opinions of this as you go.

It's as well to reassure the customer that her replies will be treated in confidence. Many people would rather not divulge for example, details of the amounts they spend.

Example of market survey result sheet

1	b	a	b	b	b
2	Tesco	Spar	Sainsbury	Safeway	FineFare
3	a	be	ac	cd	ae
4	£25	£15	£30	£40	£23
5	W/Line	Spar	—	—	VG
6	£12	£15	—	—	£6
7	abd	abd	be	be	ab
8	b	c	a	a	b
9	adf	adef	—	—	ad
10	b	bc	bcef	bcdef	bdef
11	prefer butcher	use butcher & greengrocer	—	dirty	Too dear
12	cheaper	—	cheaper	—	cheaper
13	yes	no	possibly	no	yes
14	b	b	c	a	abc
15	yes	no	no	yes	yes
16	don't play	ditto	ditto	club	post
17	—	—	—	twice week	fortnightly
18	—	—	—	club	park
19	—	—	—	no	yes
20	disgusting	sexy	ooooh	not for me	good idea, I might be able to sniff them out.

Starting from Square One

If you fancy starting a business from scratch, you have the choice of an existing empty shop, or one that is built in a new development. In either case you will probably have to pay all the legal costs. Because personal circumstances, choice of trade, situation of shop, size, etc. can vary so much, all I shall attempt to do in this section is to give generalisations, and hope they will be of some use if you are thinking along these lines.

Existing Shops

These again fall into two basic types — the High Street, and the Back Street.

(1) High Street

High Street shops, if leasehold, are generally owned by companies, such as insurance companies, rather than individuals, and because of this it can sometimes take a very long time to reach a decision. One reason for this is that they are always hoping to attract one of the big household name type stores, and inevitably will give preference to them, rather than you, an unknown individual. This is why you very often see empty shops to let for a long period of time in the High Streets. It is not because there is a lack of interest or willingness of anyone to take it over, but probably because the freeholders are hanging on in the hope of catching the big fish.

If you enquire about a shop, and do not receive a speedy reply, resign yourself to the fact that you may have to wait several months before a tentative decision is reached. You will almost certainly have to pay a premium of several thousand pounds, depending on the position, plus a hefty rent. However, you will have plenty of passing trade, and if you have done your homework properly and start a business for which there is a demand in the area, and offer goods or services at competitive prices, you should succeed.

Occasionally it is possible to rent one of these shops for a short-term period only, say six months, and in these circumstances it will provide an ideal spot for trying out a new idea or business, without getting involved in costly premiums and long leases.

Sometimes these shops will have shelving and counters left in them, but if not, they can usually be purchased quite cheaply second-hand from other shops which are being refitted or closing down. Whatever equipment you buy for the shop should be able to be sold at the end of the rental periods for whatever price you paid. As far as stock is concerned, try to buy from a wholesaler or manufacturer who will agree to take back any unsold stock at the end of the period, although a 'closing down' sale at near enough cost price for the last fortnight, should clear most items.

(2) Back Street

Back Street shops are a different kettle of fish. The main trades will probably already be represented, and there would almost certainly not be enough custom to go round if you opened in opposition. In these secondary positions there is not usually enough passing trade to support any other type of shop. Of course, if your main business comes from outside — mail order etc., or if you want the shop for a 'front' and storage area for your job of television repairs, plumbers, etc., they are a good bet, providing you can get in cheaply enough. These are also good positions for a specialist type of shop to which you will be hoping to attract your customers mainly from regular advertising in specialist publications.

Offers for all empty shops should be made in the normal manner, and if the lease is a new one being specially created, it is worth while suggesting a lower rent, or longer periods between revisions, or both.

New Developments

These usually take even longer than High Street shops to get into, because you have the same initial problems, plus the length of time it takes to build the shells, and then the added further wait whilst the shop is finished off and fitted out.

Some developments ask for tenders to be received by a certain date. These may state that there will be no premium to get in, or they may ask for a general tender in which you will have to decide how much premium you are prepared to pay, as well as the amount of rent. The length of lease and revision periods may have already been decided on. Before making any decision as to how much to offer, it is essential that you find out to what stage exactly the unit will be finished off, so that you may add the building costs to your calculations. Enquire about the following:

Floor Will it be finished and tiled, or will it be left screeded, or will it have to be screeded?

Ceiling Will the ceiling be finished including light fittings, or will you have to fit a suspended ceiling and the electrics for lighting?

Shopfront Will there be one installed, or do you have to pay for it?

Walls Will they be finished, plastered and emulsioned, or will you have to pay for this?

Plumbing What exactly will be provided?

Electrics Will any electrical fittings be installed?

You will have to obtain planning permission for a shopfront, and the landlord's consent and approval for any alterations you may wish to do. On top of this you will have to buy shelving, counters, cash registers and all other ancillary equipment needed for your particular trade. As you can see from the above, what at first may have seemed a cheap exercise, 'getting into a new shop for nothing', may turn out to be very expensive, and before committing yourself you should find out exactly what the total cost is likely to be, and equate that against your envisaged turnover. Some new developments are well worth while, others of which you probably know several, are 'white elephants'. Be sure in your own mind before signing on the dotted line. Bear in mind also, that in the case of a new shop on a new housing development, there may be quite a delay, perhaps a couple of years, between your opening the shop and the last dwelling being occupied. You will have to wait until then to realise your full potential, and be able to survive in the meantime!

It may be worth your while calling into your local Department of Employment explaining what you intend doing, and asking if there are any government schemes in operation that may be of help to you, such as 'The Enterprise Allowance Scheme', which started in August 1983, and provided an allowance of £40 per week for up to 52 weeks if you had the necessary qualifications.

Franchises

Wimpey Bars, Dyno Rod, Pronuptia, Budget Van Hire, British School of Motoring, Home Tune, Midas Exhaust Centres — all well-known names, and all were available as franchises. Unfortunately, for every one of the real successes, there are many many more that will either not make the grade, or will not give you as good an income as if you worked the same number of hours for someone else, and invested your money elsewhere.

This country is following America with regards to franchising, where it has had tremendous success. There are more and more franchises becoming available ranging in price from around £2,000 to £3,000 up to £250,000 or more. Finance against these figures is usually offered, sometimes up to 70 per cent, but care should be taken to leave sufficient working capital, if this course is taken.

In return for being allowed to use the company's name and know-how (they should have ironed out all the difficulties), you will have to make regular payments commensurate with your turnover, and pay all the normal running costs, including staff. Whatever profit is left belongs to you. The only recommendations I can give with regard to franchising are:

(1) Ask yourself why the company chooses to expand in this manner, rather than employing staff themselves.
(2) Ask your solicitor to go through the franchise agreement carefully, and let you know exactly what you are letting yourself in for.
(3) Ask an accountant to look through any company accounts available, and any projected figures given to you.
(4) Ask for a list of other franchisees, contact one or two of your own choice, and see what they have to say.
(5) Ask your bank to get a reference, and write off for trade references.
(6) If the company services various outlets in some manner, call round and try to get the customers' viewpoints.
(7) Find out the exact area you will be given, and ask if anyone else at present or in the future will be allowed to operate there also.
(8) If you are asked for any money, find out if it is returnable if for any reason you decide not to proceed.
(9) If at all possible, armed with the leaflets the company has sent you, do a 'trial run', to get an accurate response and discover the drawbacks.
(10) If you have any doubts at all, *DO NOT GO AHEAD*.

The Professionals: Choosing and Using

This section deals with the 'heavy' side of purchasing a business; the part where the professionals take over and scrutinise their own particular aspects of the business you have chosen, in order to protect your interests as far as possible. They will ensure that the business legally becomes yours, that you are aware of any immediate expenditure needed on the property according to the conditions of the lease, and that the accounts are healthy, and if accurate, will show a decent profit.

Specimen accounts and leases are shown for information purposes only, and are not intended to turn you into an expert in these fields. We shall start first with the professionals themselves.

These are the people on whom you will be relying during your business career, and whose wisdom you may question, but never ignore. Being professionals they all have the necessary qualifications, but not necessarily the business experience. So choose with care.

As an example, many years ago I sold a newsagent's shop, and used a local solicitor who was recommended to me by one of my customers. On the completion day the stocktaker asked the purchaser if he were going to take over the outstanding weekly news accounts. He replied that he did not want to. I had assumed that this contingency had been covered in the contract, and telephoned my solicitor to confirm. He told me that he had not realised that there would be any book debts, not having dealt with the sale of a newsagent's before, and there was nothing now that could be done. That mistake cost me quite a few pounds, plenty of arguments, and an eventual kidnapping of the accounts book to try and salvage some of the money owed to me. But that is another story.

Solicitors

Recommendation is the best method of finding a solicitor, although they all have to undergo a thorough training, and be fully insured against professional negligence. However, some solicitors concentrate on house conveyancing, some on divorce, others on criminal cases, etc., and many have very little experience of business transactions. In the majority of cases this will not be a problem, especially if you are experienced yourself and can foresee the problems, but if you are not, you would be advised to find a solicitor who is.

Your solicitor will also advise you at a later stage, about the small print in any agreement or contract you may be asked to sign in connection with a leasing or hire purchase agreement. Remember, every word entered in one of these contracts or agreements has been selected by the opposite party to protect themselves and give as many advantages as possible. If you do not understand the full meaning and implications of every sentence, get your solicitor to explain all the drawbacks to you. You may be unpleasantly surprised, because they seem to have a knack of translating the most harmless sounding sentence into one full of the most onerous consequences.

Accountants

If you form a *company* you will be required by law to employ a qualified accountant to prepare the annual report and accounts. If a *sole trader* or *partnership*, you are not required to have an accountant, and if you do, he need not have any qualifications. Although some people in this category achieve a high degree of competency, you are advised to choose an accountant who is a member of one of the accountants' associations, and who will be subject to its disciplinary rules. The two main associations are the Institute of Chartered Accountants, and the Association of Certified Accountants.

The *Chartered* Accountant is the most highly qualified, uses the letters FCA or ACA, and generally charges the highest fees.

The *Certified* Accountant is slightly less qualified than the 'chartered' and uses the initials FACCA or AACCA.

The *Registered* Accountant has the lowest qualifications and usually charges the lowest fees.

As far as choosing an accountant is concerned, your best bet is again to follow the advice of someone in business, and then ask the accountant for an estimate, or a scale of charges, before commissioning him. It is as well to be prepared.

How to complain If you have a complaint about an accountant, and he is a member of the Royal Institution of Chartered Accountants, write to; RICA, Chartered Accountants Hall, PO Box 433, Moorgate Place, London EC2P 2BJ. If the accountant is not chartered, but is registered, write to The Complaints Investigation Committee, The Society of Company and Commercial Accountants, 11 Portland Road, Edsgbaston, Birmingham B16 9HN.

Surveyors

Always use a *Chartered* surveyor. If you then have any complaints against him, you can complain to: The Secretary for Professional Practice, Royal Institute of Chartered Surveyors, 12 Great George Street, Parliament Square, London SW1P 3AD.

Stocktakers

If you arrange for your stock to be valued by a stocktaker, find out details of how their fees are based, and whether there is a minimum charge. It will often pay to shop around.

Banking

If you are trading as a small trader you are best advised to have two separate bank accounts, one for the business, and one for your personal use. They can be headed 'T. Jones — Private Account', and 'T. Jones — Business Account' or the trading name of the shop if you trade under another name. You will than have two cheque books and two paying-in books. It is best if you pay your drawings into the private account on a regular basis - weekly, fortnightly or monthly. Your 'drawings' is the salary you pay yourself, and should be used for personal and household items. By using this method you will not be tempted to spend more than you earn — you will be surprised how easily this can be done. With regard to this last point, bear in mind that you will have to pay income tax at the end of the financial year, and provision should be made for this. *NOT* allowing for this is one of the major contributions to shop bankruptcies — being forced to sell to pay off the Inland Revenue tax debt.

Your first step then, is to open a bank account. This is usually arranged before you take over the business, and will certainly be done if you are arranging a bank loan.

There are two types of bank account — current and deposit. Your business account will be run off a current account, which does not pay interest, and on which you will pay bank charges which will be worked out to a formula of your own bank, and is based on the amount of work the bank does on your account, less a figure based on your average credit balance. It is worth discussing with your bank manager, the average amount needed in your account to offset bank charges, considering your own type of business, and how much work the bank will have to do.

If you have more money in your current account than is needed for your day-to-day requirements, or to cover any bank charges, the excess should be transferred to a deposit account, where it will earn interest. This interest has to be declared at the end of the year for tax purposes. If any extra money is needed in your current account, this can be achieved immediately by giving written instructions to your bank to transfer 'x' amount of pounds from your deposit account to your current account.

Do not have an overdraft on your current account, and a credit balance on an investment account, because you will be charged more interest on your overdraft than you will earn on the investment account.

Overdrafts are only short-term loans, although they may be continually revised or extended, and are the cheapest form of borrowed money. Most businessmen either have a continual overdraft or are faced with the fact that they have to have one at various stages of their business life. There is nothing shameful about having an overdraft, especially if by using this facility you are able to purchase goods at a much lower price, and thus make more savings than the interest you are being charged on the overdraft.

There is a very simple method of calculating this. First, ask your bank manager how much interest would be payable on a £1,000 overdraft. This is the amount you will have to pay *per year*. Divide by 52, and now you have the weekly cost. If you can save more than this per week by buying differently then go ahead and earn some extra money, and increase your gross profit percentage. Your bank manager may ask for additional security, and if the overdraft requested is for a larger amount he will probably have to ask for Head office approval, which may take some time.

If you make any promises to a bank manager regarding repayment of loans or overdrafts, ensure you keep them. You never know when you will need another.

Bank charges If your bank charges seem excessive, do not be afraid to confront your bank manager and ask for a breakdown of the figures. You may be able to agree a new basis for charges, or be able to alter the way you conduct your affairs, and thus reduce your costs. If you are unable to achieve this, you still retain the option of enquiring from another bank as to how they would assess their charges.

The Accounts

Sole Trader

Trading and Profit and Loss Account for the Year ended 19th August 1987.

SALES	161,937
Stock at 20.8.86	6,125
Purchases	128,275
	134,400
Less Stock at 19.8.87	7,426
COST OF SALES	126,974
GROSS PROFIT (21.6%)	34,963
Overhead Expenses:	
Rent and Rates	3,058
Light and Heat	1,017
Telephone	166
Insurance	213
Bank Charges	210
Repairs, Renewals and Maintenance	265
Postage, Printing, Stationery and Advertising	62
Bags and Labels	835
Vehicle Expenses	1,542
Wages	11,792
Cleaning	239
Sundry Trade Expenses	445
Accountancy	495
Rental of Security Equipment	410
Hire Purchase Interest	476
Leasing of Equipment	341
Depreciation	1,512
TOTAL OVERHEADS	23,078
NET PROFIT (7.46%)	11,885

Balance Sheet as at 19 August 1987

	1982
CURRENT ASSETS	
Stock as valued by propreitor	7,426
Debtors	2,551
Cash at Bank	586
Cash in Hand	606
	11,169

CURRENT LIABILITIES

Creditors	6,132
Bank Overdraft	662
	6,794

NET CURRENT ASSETS   4,375

FIXED ASSETS	Goodwill	Fixtures, Fittings, & Equipment	Motor Vehicle	TOTAL	
Net book values at 20.8.86	5,000	2,137	2,717	9,854	
Additions	—	825	963	1,788	
	5,000	2,962	3,680	11,642	
Depreciation	—	592	920	1,512	
Net Book Values at 19.8.87	5,000	2,370	2,760	10,130	10,130
					14,505

CAPITAL

at 20.8.86	14,056	
Add profit for year	11,885	
	25,941	
Less Drawings During Year	11,436	
	14,505	14,505

If you are satisfied with the general appearance, location and accommodation of the shop, the next thing to check is the accounts. This is the most important single item on the agenda, because the sales figures shown on the accounts will largely determine the value of the business, and this figure, together with the gross and net figures, will be the amounts your bank will need to know if you desire a loan. They will of course, need to study copies of at least the last three years' accounts, and if there is any problem in providing current accounts, you are advised to start looking for another business immediately. ALL businesses have to provide accounts to the Inland Revenue every year. This is how the amount of income tax payable is calculated. If no accounts are submitted to the tax office, the Inland Revenue will make an assessment of tax payable which is deliberately high, and usually will not take into account all your tax allowances. As nobody likes paying more tax than is essential, an appeal is made against the assessment either by the owner of the business or his accountant, and a proper set of accounts is then submitted to allow the tax office to review the situation, and reduce the amount payable. You should always appeal against an assessment, even if it is correct, because once the final figure has been agreed 'on appeal' it is final. If you just pay up, the taxman could decide at a later date that it was incorrect, and ask for more. If anyone states they do not have accounts, it probably means either the yearly takings are far short of what is currently claimed, or the gross profit or net profit is minimal, or all three. Whatever the reason, if the vendor is reticent about showing accounts, you can be sure your bank manager will not be very forthcoming.

Take no notice if a vendor states that the amount of takings shown on the accounts are less than they actually are. He has two choices. Either he shows the true figures on the accounts and obtains the full value of the business, or he saves on paying income tax by reducing his takings in the takings book, and thus reduces the value of his business. He cannot have it both ways. Your bank will not be interested in any mythical figures. They want everything in black and white, and will assume the accounts are accurate, and will base their value and amount of any loan on these. You must therefore ignore any statements from the vendor telling you how much extra he takes a week that 'isn't shown'. If in the event, this happens to be true, all well and good, you can count it as something extra you had not expected, but on no account pay for it initially by paying a higher price for the business than the accounts warrant.

A husband and wife have the choice of trading as a Sole Trader or as a Partnership. If they trade as a sole trader, the wife should be given a wage which is shown on the yearly accounts.

If they trade as a Partnership, a wife cannot be paid a wage, because she wil receive her income from the net profit of the business. A point to bear in mind is that if the business is sold, any gain is divided between partners and each is able to claim the capital gains annual exemption of £6,600 (1987/88). If the business is run as a Sole Trader, only ONE person can claim the exemption.

The following notes are to help you understand the way in which accounts are set out. In your interests it is best to have a qualified accountant study them and give his opinion.

If it is possible to see five years accounts, do so. I am sorry to keep harping back to the fact that you must, if not actually suspect the vendor of misrepresentation or the deliberate hiding of certain facts, certainly check every avenue you possibly can. The reason for asking to see as many past accounts as possible is to allow you to get as complete a picture as possible of how the shop has been run and its performance over the past few years. The following table gives an example of how to do this.

Performance figures

	1983	1984	1985	1986	1987
Sales	111,039	122,601	135,847	151,768	161,937
Stock	3,812	4,296	5,541	6,125	7,426
Gross Profit	18,016	21,699	26,672	30,830	34,963
GP%	16.22	17.69	19.63	20.31	21.59
Net Profit	6,508	6,415	8,680	11,404	12,081
Net Profit %	5.86	5.23	6.38	7.51	7.46
Rent & Rates	1,702	1,666	2,804	3,011	3,058
Light & Heat	885	849	1,007	962	1,017
Telephone	111	129	204	211	166
Insurance	104	123	124	123	210
Bank Charges	104	—	—	—	213
Repairs Renovations and Maintenance	176	913	907	506	265
Postage stationery, advertising	142	32	199	149	62
Bags and Labels	—	422	690	741	835
Vehicle Expenses	617	732	758	896	1,542
Wages	5,148	6,281	7,456	8,747	11,792
Wages as % of sales	4.6	5.1	5.4	5.7	7.2
Cleaning	266	343	388	399	141
Sundry Expenses	726	618	270	426	445
Accountancy	300	380	400	450	495
Rental of security equipment	334	410	410	410	410
Hire Purchase Interest	—	206	494	583	476
Depreciation	493	1,906	1,576	1,440	1,512
TOTAL OVERHEADS	11,508	15,410	18,012	19,426	22,980
DRAWINGS	3,797	6,663	6,796	9,364	11,632

From this you will notice if there has been any sudden increase or decrease in sales, gross profit margins, wages, etc. Incidentally, if the gross profit percentage is not shown on the accounts, as in the majority of cases it is very simple to calculate. Just divide the amount of gross profit by the total sales figures and multiply by 100.

$$\frac{\text{Gross Profit} \times 100}{\text{Sales}} = \text{GP\%}$$

You will also notice that there is a gradual increase in expenses over the years. This is perfectly natural, and is due to inflation. Minimum staff wages are set by Wages Councils each year, and should also show a steady increase. If they do not, it means that there are fewer staff employed than previously, or that they are working shorter hours.

This also means that the vendor has had to work harder, and is a possible cause of the shop being put up for sale. Gross profit should also show a steady increase (inflation again), but the gross profit percentage should remain pretty much the same. If this percentage drops dramatically, it could mean that to keep the sales figures high, a lot of cut-pricing has been done, or it could be thieving by customers and/or staff, or deliberate 'milking' of the till by the vendor. It could also be a miscalculation of the annual stock, but if this were the case, the percentage should be higher the following year. Careful note should also be taken of the sales figures. It has been known for a vendor who intends selling the business in, say two years or so, to push up these figures in order to obtain a higher price for the business, regardless of having to pay more income tax for a couple of years. If there is a sudden increase in sales, remember that in order to take this extra money, more staff would be needed, more bags, paper, till rolls, etc., as well as possibly, more equipment such as extra tills or scales. Therefore look to see if there has been a corresponding increase in these amounts also.

Now to study the actual accounts shown on pages 38 to 39 in more detail. They are divided up into three sections. The Trading Account, the Profit and Loss Account, and The Balance Sheet. They all apply to a sole trader.

(1) The Trading Account

Sometimes this is shown separately, and sometimes as the first part of the 'Trading and Profit and Loss Account' as shown in the example. It shows the total value of the stock at cost price at the start of the year, the value of the stock at the end of the year, and the amount of stock purchased throughout the year. This will give the total cost of all goods purchased during the year, and when this figure is deducted from the total sales as shown, will give the gross profit for the year. Gross profit then, is the difference between the buying and selling prices of all your goods, not taking into account any of the expenses necessary in the running of the shop. The gross profit percentage should be compared with the norm for that type of shop, and if it is abnormally high or low, the reason looked for. Higher than normal gross profits may be due to high prices being charged generally, or a large percentage of the turnover being in a high profit line, or the opening stock value being undervalued, or the final stock value being overvalued. Although the accounts may be prepared by an accountant, the actual stocktaking is usually done by the vendor, and is not checked. It is possible for him to misrepresent the stock value, and consequently improve the gross profit percentage. In the example given, if the final stock at 19.8.87 were increased by £2,000 to £9,426, the gross profit would be increased to £36,963 or 22 per cent.

(2) The Profit and Loss Account

The purpose of this account is to offset the various business expenses against the gross profit, and thus end up with a *net* profit. There are no hard and fast rules for this section, because it is up to the individual shopkeeper to spend his money where he places most emphasis, or not at all. For instance, in two identical shops, one proprietor may not wish to work more than two days a week, and has a wage bill double the other. Or one spends a fortune advertising, the other nothing at all. Although the items are self-explanatory, we shall go through them briefly one by one.

Rent: When working out the profitability of the shop, take into account the date when the next rent renewal or review occurs, and if this is within the next year or so, be sure to allow for a sufficient increase in this figure, especially if it is some years since a review, when the rent could easily double or even treble.

Rates: These are charged by the local authority and Water Board in the same manner as for ordinary houses, except at a higher rate, and invariably rise every year in the same way. They will also be increased if any additions are made to the premises. Bear in mind also that rate reductions may be applied for, if there is a loss of trade through nearby developments or adverse conditions. We were once granted a ten per cent reduction in our rates after we complained that a local factory estate had laid off hundreds of people, and also that a new bus service had been introduced which made people walk away from the shop, instead of queuing outside. One point to bear in mind — check with your neighbours first to enquire how much they are paying, and how their premises compare to yours, or you could find yourself faced with a rates increase instead when the rating officer arrives to check. A ten per cent reduction may not seem much, but if you could reduce all your expenses by an average of ten per cent, it would mean for instance an extra £44 per week on the specimen accounts shown.

Light and Heat: Determine whether or not there are separate meters for the accommodation and the shop, and if the amount shown on the accounts is for the shop alone. If it includes an amount for home use do not be misled by the vendor into thinking that it is all offset against tax. What will probably happen, is that when the Inspector of Taxes comes to compute your personal tax payable, he will add back a certain amount for home use. This will also happen with the telephone and vehicle expense amounts.

Telephone: See above

Insurance: This is comprised of a combination of shopkeeper's insurance, and building insurance. *Shopkeeper's* insurance is for fixtures and fittings, stock, public liability, shop windows, etc., and is at his discretion. If he wishes, he may not be insured at all for these items, if he is willing to take the risk himself. *Buildings* insurance will be compulsory on leasehold premises, arranged by the freeholder, who will usually ask for the annual premium to be paid to him with an appropriate quarter's rent. If the building is freehold, the insurance will be insisted upon by the mortgagor, just as with private houses.

Bank Charges: Self-explanatory. They do give some sort of guide to the vendor's financial position, although this figure may be due to something entirely different.

Repairs, Renewals and Maintenance: A note should be kept of all monies spent on the premises. It is very easy to forget the odd tin of paint, etc., but these are all tax-deductible and should be entered in the book. Note should also be taken of the amount of money that has been spent on the premises over the last few years. If this is negligible, and the property is old, it is quite likely that you will have to spend money on it in the near future.

Postage, Printing, etc: Self-explanatory.

Bags and Labels: Self-explanatory.

Vehicle Expenses: See 'Light and Heat' above.

Wages: Get a breakdown of the number of staff and how much they are paid, and then see if the total wage bill includes an amount for the vendor's wife. If so, this figure may be added back to the net profit, for practical purposes. The reason for entering the wife's wages in the accounts is to save tax. It works like this. Every person is allowed to earn up to a certain wage without paying tax or NI. If this amount were added to the husband's net profit instead of being listed as his wife's wages, he would have to pay tax on the total amount, possibly about £500, which would be completely unnecessary. Do not believe the vendor if he states that the wage bill includes his own salary. His salary is the net profit. If he withdraws a certain amount each week, it will be shown as 'drawings'.

Cleaning: This is usually window cleaning, or for a contractor who comes in to clean the floor and/or equipment, not necessarily on a regular basis.

Sundry Trade Expenses: Covers a multitude of sins, from drawings pins to lavatory paper, and from dish cloths to felt tip markers.

Accountancy: A good accountant will save more than his fee, in income tax, apart from the hours of work involved, to start with at least. It becomes debatable after a time however, if profits decrease and his fees increase annually.

Rental of Security Equipment: Or rental of anything connected with the business. These rental payments may be offset in their entirety for tax purposes, and on occasions can prove advantageous, particularly as a minimal initial cash payment is required. Find out exactly what is on rental, the number of years remaining, and the cost of the payments. Then find out what the vendor intends doing about them. If he intends clearing them up, this amount may be added to the net profit.

Hire Purchase Interest: Tax relief may be gained on the interest part of anything bought on hire purchase for the shop. Find out what equipment is on hire purchase, and the length of the remaining term, and what the vendor's intentions are regarding these. If he clears it off as above, this figure may be added to the net profit also.

Leasing of Equipment: Similar to 'renting' above.

Depreciation: This is the amount by which the fixtures, fittings, and vehicle costs are devalued each year. The theory is that all equipment has only a limited life, and sufficient funds are retained to replace when necessary. There are various ways of doing this, but your accountant will choose the one best suited for you. Depreciation is a 'book figure', and in reality can be added back to the net profit when deciding how much one can earn from a particular business.

Net Profit: This is the most important part of the accounts, because it shows the amount of money you should be left with after paying all the expenses connected with the shop. It is also the figure your bank manager will be most interested in, to see how much you can repay. As said above, a true net figure may be obtained by adding back various 'paper' expenses, such as wife's wages, HP Interest, depreciation, etc.

(3) The Balance Sheet

This third part shows the financial position of the business. It gives figures for the amount of money owing to the business, and owed by the business, as well as the current cash situation.

Current Assets: This is self-explanatory. Items are usually listed with cash at the bottom. The nearer the asset is to cash, the lower it is placed.

Current Liabilities: Creditors are firms to whom money is owed for goods or services which have been supplied with a relatively short period of credit. The figure shown in the accounts is the cumulative total of all monies outstanding to these firms on the day stocktaking was done. Banks and building societies which have granted loans and mortgages are not counted as creditors. Overdrafts are always given with an upper limit.

Fixed Assets

Goodwill is an intangible asset. It is not something that could be sold separately if the shop lost all its trade — like the fixtures and fittings, or motor car, or the residue of the lease. It is in fact related to the amount of trade that has been built up in the shop over the years, and is the result of getting established and well known in the district, and of conducting the business in a fair and honest manner, in a shop that is clean and attractive and sufficiently well stocked.

In practice it is determined when the business is sold, and the purchase price is apportioned between Fixtures and Fittings, Lease, and Goodwill, by the accountant, who will try to arrange the three figures in such a way as will benefit the vendor most with regard to Capital Gains Tax and Income Tax. The figure for Goodwill then in the accounts, bears no relevance to anything, apart from the fact that that was the amount apportioned to it when the vendor bought the business. There are no additions, nor depreciation values, because as already mentioned, this figure will be decided upon by the vendor with his accountant, when a price for the shop has been agreed. In other words, if the shop has done badly since he bought it, the goodwill entered in the accounts will be more than that eventually apportioned, and on the other hand, if the shop turnover has improved tremendously without much money being spent on new fixtures and fittings, the new goodwill figure will be considerably more. One also has to take into account the length of time the vendor has been in occupation.

Fixtures, Fittings and Equipment This figure, again, is based upon the initial apportionment when the shop was bought, and any new purchases during the year are added to it. *Additions* are only for new additional items, or existing ones that are replaced. They are not for repairs to existing equipment.

Depreciation: the rate of this is decided with income tax in mind. See 'Depreciation' in Profit and Loss Account.

Motor Vehicle: This again is for capital expenditure — not for items such as petrol, oil, and servicing. Depreciation is as above.

The *total* depreciation values of Fixtures and Fittings, and Motor Vehicles, are carried forward to the Profit and Loss Account.

Drawings: This is an interesting figure, because it shows how much the vendor has officially withdrawn from the business during the year.

Partnerships

The accounts for a partnership are almost exactly the same as for a sole trader, the difference being, as mentioned previously, that a sole trader is the proprietor, and that if the business is run by two or more people, it becomes a partnership. The accounts must therefore show each partner's capital and drawings in the final accounts. Partnerships may be comprised of friends, relations, or husbands and wives, and division of profits may be on an equal basis, or any other formula agreed upon. Examples are now given of two equal partners, and of an unequal one, between perhaps a husband and wife, for tax purposes. They follow on from the previous accounts, and are in every way similar except for the method of displaying the net profit, drawings, and capital, and must be in accordance with any Partnership Agreement that has been drawn up.

The following entries would replace the 'Net Profit' and 'Capital' in the example accounts.

(1) EQUAL PARTNERS

Profit and Loss Account
Share of Profit

Mr A Jones	5,943	
Mr T Smith	5,942	
	11,885	

Balance Sheet

CAPITAL	Mr A Jones	Mr T Smith	
at 20.8.86	8,239	5,817	
Add share of profit	5,943	5,942	
	14,182	11,759	
Less drawings	5,055	6,381	
	9,127	5,378	14,505

(2) UNEQUAL PARTNERS

Profit and Loss Account
Share of Profit

Mr A Jones — two thirds	7,924	
Mrs S Jones — one third	3,961	
	11,885	

Balance Sheet

CAPITAL	Mr A Jones	Mrs S Jones	
20.8.86	9,371	4,685	
Add share of profit	7,924	3,961	
	17,295	8,646	
Less drawings	7,624	3,812	
	9,671	4,834	14,505

The previous examples are self-explanatory. Number 2 is an alternative method for husbands and wives to use, instead of adding a wage for the wife to the total wage bill. *Note* — both methods cannot be used at the same time. You cannot claim wages for a partner. The partner's salary comes from the net profit.

Limited Companies

As this is not a book intended to turn you into an accountant, and as
the sale of a small shop which also happens to be a limited company
occurs so infrequently, I shall only make a brief reference to the
accounts. Your accountant will advise and explain these to you far
more quickly and better than pages of words.

Briefly, if you are purchasing a limited company, you can buy the
'Trade and Fixed Assets', or you can buy the 'Share Capital'. If you
buy the former you will not be responsible or liable for any debts that
have occurred prior to your purchase. If you buy the latter the reverse
is true, but you will be able to trade under the name of the existing
company, having bought the shares.

The Profit and Loss Account will show the same expenses as for a
Sole Trader, apart from the fact that the director's salary will be shown
separately as Director's Remuneration.

There is also a Profit and Loss (Appropriation) Account which deals
with Final Dividends and Corporation Tax.

The Balance Sheet, apart from the usual Fixed and Current Assets
and Liabilities, deals with the company shares.

Some Useful Terms and what they mean

Working Capital is the amount of money needed to enable you to pay
all your bills, whether for stock or general expenses such as rent, rates,
electricity, etc., when they become due. From the time that you take
over a business you will have cash coming in, in the form of takings,
and your bank balance will start to grow. Do not make the mistake of
rushing out to buy a new car or have the kitchen completely refitted
with this money, because it will be needed to replace the stock you
have just sold, and also meet the next instalments of rates, rent, etc.
After about six months you should have a pretty good idea of how
much working capital you need in order to pay all your bills and
general expenses on time.

Working Capital Ratio is the proportion of your current assets, as
opposed to your current liabilities. Current Assets are items such as
stock, cash at the bank and in hand, and debtors — in other words,
assets which can quickly be turned into cash. Current libilities are of
course, your debts. If you have assets of £1,000, and liabilities of
£1,000, the ratio would be 1:1. This would be just about sufficient. To
be in a healthy position, the ratio would need to be larger than this,
perhaps 2:1, which would mean current assets of £2,000 and liabilities
of £1,000. To arrive at your own ratio, divide your current assets by
your current liabilities.

Over-capitalisation is when too much of your money is tied up in buildings, equipment, etc. (fixed assets), and you are left with insufficient working capital, so that to be able to continue trading you may have to arrange a bank loan or overdraft facilities, which of course will take some of your profit in interest charges.

Liquid Capital means cash, ready money. Your stock cannot be counted as this because it is not able to be readily changed into cash. Liquid capital is what is left after deducting the value of your stock from your current assets.

Over-trading This is when your liquid capital is not sufficient to pay all your liabilities if all your creditors wished to be paid at once. It is possible therefore, for a business to have a healthy *working capital*, but still be *over-trading*, and in fact, many many shops come into this category.

We shall now put the above into practice with our fictitious accounts, and see how they stand the test.

Working Capital Ratio: Current assets £11,169. Current liabilities £6,794. 11,169/6,794 = 1.64:1 a fairly healthy position.

Liquid Capital: 11,169 — 7,426 (stock) = 3,743. Liabilities 6,794. As there is not enough Liquid Capital to clear all the Current Liabilities the shop is overtrading.

Accounts: Current Period

Attention must be paid to the date the last accounts were made up to. If they are very recent, say up to three months old, the accounts should be a good guide to the current trading position, but if they are older, they may have changed dramatically since that time, due to local environmental changes or other causes. If they *have* changed, you can be sure it will be for the worse. The purpose of this section of the book is to describe some of the methods you can use to check, as far as possible, the most recent takings and profits.

(1) Accounts over 14 months old

If the latest accounts are well over a year old, it could mean one of two things. Either the vendor is very slow in making up his books and sending them to his accountant, which would make me question the accuracy of his figures, or his accountant is particularly slow in preparing them. If the fault lies with the vendor, it does not augur very well for the business, because anyone placing his shop on the market knows full well that all prospective purchasers will wish to study the accounts, and will definitely need them for their bank if they are applying for a loan. It could very well be then, that they have not been made up because the trade has declined to such an extent during the past year that it has altered the profits, and therefore the value of the business. If this situation coincides with some new local opposition, yellow lines, etc., my advice is to steer clear, and start looking for a shop again elsewhere. Most people have no idea of how quickly trade can disappear in adverse conditions. In the space of two months takings could be slaughtered. If none of these events appears to have taken place, and you are still interested, you will have to insist on the accounts being prepared immediately, and made available to you as soon as possible. The length of time this takes will depend on whether the accountant has all the relevant paperwork or not. If he has, you could have the accounts in a week. If the vendor has not finished preparing the books to send to his accountant, you may have to wait at least a month, and then some time after that to get a decision from a bank.

(2) Accounts between 3 months and 14 months

During this period it is possible for the trade to have altered considerably also. It will be necessary, therefore, to carry out a number of checks on the business to try and ascertain the current position. This assumes that the vendor maintains a cash book in which is recorded the daily takings, and also the various payments to suppliers, and other outgoings. It means having access to the cash book, the bank statements, and the invoices and expenses, for a few hours. Do not be frightened to ask for these. After all, the vendor is asking you to pay him several thousand pounds for the privilege of buying his business, and you are entitled to investigate it in a proper manner. And it is the easiest thing in the world to enter fictitious figures in a cash book. You must check the following:

(a) Bank Statements and Cash Book Reconciliation Check that all amounts shown as banked in the cash book appear on the statements, and tick them off with a pencil on both sheets. While doing this, make sure also that the amount banked agrees with the weekly takings, less any cash purchases and expenses such as wages. If there is no amount entered in the cash book as banked, you will have to do this anyway. Having worked your way through the period in question, go back to the beginning and ask the vendor for explanations for items appearing in one and not the other. It would be particularly suspect if several amounts shown as banked in the cash book do not appear on the statements. These could be fictitious entries to substantiate the takings.

Do the above exercise with regard to purchases and expenses. The thing to look out for here, is the reverse of the above. That is, amounts shown on the statements, but not in the cash book. These would of course, give a false impression of the business by improving the gross profit, and explanations for these should be sought from the vendor.

If all the cash book entries agree with the bank statements, you can assume the cash book is correct.

(b) Comparison with Past Accounts Total all the weekly takings, purchases, and expenses separately, and compare with the last available accounts. For instance, if the period in question is for eight months, these figures should be roughly equivalent to two-thirds of those shown on the accounts. They will not be exact because of inflation and seasonal variations, but should give a good guide to the current trading position once these factors have been taken into account.

(c) Current Stock Position and Liabilities If there is a discrepancy in the purchases and expenses totals in (b), it could be that the level of stock held at the moment is different to the average of the past year, or that the liabilities are now higher.

In trades where the stock can be easily counted, such as a butcher's, or where several large items may account for the majority of the stock, such as an electrical shop, a quick store check should be carried out, and compared to the closing stock figure on the last accounts. In other cases you can only hazard a guess. If the shop and stock area is completely filled with goods for sale, you can assume that the current stock level will not be less than that shown previously. If it is half empty you can assume the reverse — it will not be more than on the accounts.

Liabilities of both purchases and expenses may be checked also to a degree by following the payment patterns for different suppliers, to see which are still outstanding, and following the same procedure for rent, rates, etc.

Having made a shrewd estimate on the state of the stock and liabilities, this can now be amalgamated with all the previous figures, and an up-to-date statement of accounts prepared, to indicate the gross profit.

If the vendor has no details, or refuses to allow you to check on the above items — forget it!

Income Tax

We have already mentioned the fact that some vendors will either openly state, or intimate, that they withdraw a certain amount of cash regularly from the takings, which is not shown on the accounts, and on which they do not pay income tax. We have also stated that you should take no notice of this, and certainly not pay any extra for the business because of it. In fact it is very doubtful that this does go on to any great extent, particularly nowadays with pinched profit margins, and sales which are far from buoyant. In smaller businesses, where net profits are not all that high, it would be a pointless exercise anyway. The Inland Revenue have a set scale of percentages of gross profit for each type of business, and if any accounts are submitted showing a substantially lower profit margin, they are liable to be involved in a lengthy and costly investigation, probably ending up with several past years' accounts under scrutiny, and the distinct possibility of a hefty bill for back tax.

On several occasions, looking at shops for sale, the vendors have told us that the business is really much more profitable than it appears, because they take £30 or so, out of the till for spending money each day. Looking at it sensibly, this would be £180 per week, or over £9,000 per year off the sales total, which is the equivalent of a 17 per cent decrease in gross profit on takings of £1,000 per week, an 8 per cent decrease on £2,000 per week, and a 5½ per cent decrease on £3,000 per week takings. You will notice that the percentage drop is much larger on the smallest turnover, but even on the largest it is a sufficient amount to warrant an investigation by the Inland Revenue. As they are currently investigating businesses which are showing near-normal profits for their various trades, it is far better to show all your takings, and make absolutely sure you remember to enter all your expenses, so that they may be offset against the taxable figure. Bear in mind that apart from asking for back tax, there is also a severe fine and possible imprisonment for tax avoidance if the case is proved in favour of the Inland Revenue. However, I believe this problem is vastly exaggerated, and is really practically non-existent in the smaller business, for, after a wife's wage allowance of approximately £2,000, and various personal allowances have been deducted, there would not be a great deal to pay anyway.

The vendor may tell you that he lives rent free, and charges all rates, heat and light, telephone and vehicle expenses, to the business. A look at the accounts will, on the surface, confirm this, because the total amount of rent and rates, etc., will be charged against the gross profit figure.

In actual fact, this is not so. It depends on whether the vendor lives on the premises or not, and on several other factors. A proportion of each of these expenses will be added back to the net profit by the Inland Revenue for any which they consider constitute private as well as business use. Usually they are quite lenient in this respect.

There now follows a personal taxation breakdown on the example accounts previously shown. This follows on from the net profit figure of £11,885.

Mr Sole Trader		
Net Profit (as shown on the accounts)		11,855
Add		
Proportion of rent, rates, light, etc.	650	
Personal use of motor vehicle	650	
Depreciation of fixtures and fittings	592	
Depreciation of motor vehicle	920	2,812
		14,697
Less		
Fixtures and fittings allowance	430	
Motor car allowance	750	
Personal married allowance	3,795	4,975
		10,062

   Income tax would then be payable on £9,722 at the standard rate of tax, which is 27 per cent at the moment. If the tax rate were changed, the amount payable would differ, but the method of arriving at the taxable income would remain the same. Every person's individual circumstance differs, so there may be other allowances to deduct from this final figure, e.g. pension schemes or mortgage interest. There may also be other additions such as interest on investment accounts, etc.

   The reason that depreciation for fixtures and fittings, and motor cars is added back, is because there is a variety of methods of ascertaining these figures. The Inland Revenue uses a set of capital allowance scales for different classes of assets, and this is used to determine the annual capital allowance figure for each section, hence the differing values of depreciation 'added back', and capital allowances deducted.

Choice of Accounting Date

You are allowed to decide yourself the date up to which your accounts are to be made up. Your accountant will advise you on the best method to choose. You may make them up at the end of the first year's trading, and then on the same date every year afterwards, or you may choose a particular date, such as 31 December or 5 April.

   The actual income tax year runs from 6 April to the following 5 April, and is usually referred to by the two years concerned. Therefore the income tax year running from 6 April 1987 to 5 April 1988 is described as the Income Tax year 1987-88. The general rule is that the tax assessment is based on the profits of the 12 months trading account ending in the previous year of assessment.

Tax Assessments

You are required by law to make a true return of your income each year. Normally no assessments will be made until you have completed twelve months trading, but you will then receive two assessments together (covering the first two Income Tax years). The tax on the profits of a business is usually payable in two equal instalments on 1 January and 1 July. An assessment for the Income Tax year 1987-88, for example, would normally be made in the autumn of 1987 and the tax would be payable in two parts on 1 January 1988 and 1 July 1988.

If, however, you had started to trade in July 1987, for example, no assessment would be made until some time after July 1986. Assessments for both the years 1987-88 and 1988-89 would be made in the Autumn of 1986. The tax for 1987-88 would then be payable in full at the end of 30 days beginning with the date of issue of the notice of assessment and the tax for 1988-89 would be payable on 1 January and 1 July 1989.

Appeals against Assessments

If you disagree with the assessment you have 30 days in which to appeal in writing against it. In the event of your not being able to agree a figure of assessable profits with the Inspector, you will be asked to attend a meeting of the Commissioners who will make a final decision after seeing all the evidence.

Interest is chargeable on overdue tax.

Income Tax Rates 1987/88

Rate of Tax %	Taxable Income Band (£)
27	0–17,900
40	17,901–20,400
45	20,401–25,400
50	25,401–33,300
55	33,301–41,200
60	41,201 and over

Capital Gains Tax

This is payable if there is a net gain from the sale of a business. However, if you purchase another business within the period of one year before and three years after the sale of your present business, you will be entitled to 'roll over' relief. This means that the gain on the sale of the first shop is deducted from the cost of the new shop, and you do not pay tax until there is a sale and no replacement.

Retirement

When you reach retirement age and dispose of your business, you may be exempt from Capital Gains Tax on gains of up to £125,000. You can only claim the full retirement relief after you reach the age of 60 and if for the 10 years before its disposal you had owned the business or a partnership share in it, or had been a full time working director in your family trading company.

If the period is less than 10 years, you get a proportion of the full relief at the rate of £10,000 per year, but you get no relief if the period is less than one year. If you have already claimed retirement relief, your exemption limit for future claims is reduced by that amount.

If you have to retire and sell your business before the age of 60 through ill health you may still be eligible for full relief.

There is no Capital Gains Tax liability on any part of the property which is used as living accommodation by the owner. As a rule of thumb this is usually calculated as being approximately one third.

As an example, take a 60 year old man who has lived above his shop for over ten years and sells it for £244,000. He originally paid £40,000 for the business and has incurred legal fees of £3,000 in buying and selling the property. The Capital Gains Tax calculation would be as follows:

Sale of business		£244,000
Purchase Price	£40,000	
Legal Fees	3,000	43,000
		201,000
Less ⅓ owner occupation		67,000
		134,000
Full Retirement Relief	125,000	
Final Exemption	6,600	131,600
Amount Liable To Capital Gains Tax		2400

£2,400 @ 30% = £720 payable

When You Take Over . . .

The first thing you must do is contact your local Inspector of Taxes, and give full details of the business as requested. If you were previously employed you should also send him your P45 which you should have received when you left. You should also inform the local office of the Department of Health and Social Security, who will need to know for National Insurance contribution purposes.

VAT

The following information is correct at the time of going to press, but because VAT regulations are continually being altered, you are advised to seek the advice of your local VAT office before doing anything at all. They will be only too pleased to help. You will find their telephone number under 'Customs & Excise'.

All supplies of goods and services as far as VAT is concerned, are either TAXABLE or EXEMPT. An exempt supply is one on which VAT cannot be charged by law. Examples of exempt supplies are sales and leases of land and buildings, various financial and insurance dealings, some educational and health care supplies, and postage stamps.

If a supply is not exempt it is taxable. If your taxable turnover exceeds certain limits, (£21,300 p.a. or £7250 per quarter for 1987/88), you are a taxable *person* and as such must register for VAT purposes. It is the *person*, not the business who is registered for VAT, and each registration covers ALL the business activities of that *person*. So far as shops are concerned, the *person* can be a sole proprietor, a partnership, or a limited company. What is more, it is possible for a *person* to be registered as a partnership with his wife in the shop, and also run a side line as a sole proprietor. If the taxable turnover on the side line was below the VAT limits, the person would not be liable for VAT on that part of his business activities.

There are, at the moment, two rates of tax; a standard rate and a zero rate. Although there is no tax due on a zero rated supply, it should not be confused with an exempt supply. Zero rated supplies are taxable — but at 0%! The standard rate of VAT is currently 15%.

When you make a taxable supply to your customer you charge him VAT. This is called your output tax. Tax charged to you for business purposes is your input tax. At the end of your accounting period the difference between these two taxes is either paid to Customs & Excise or claimed back from them.

You can only reclaim VAT on a proper tax invoice, that is one which describes the goods and shows the VAT element. It must also show a VAT registration number, and certain other information. You cannot claim VAT on a statement. However, you can claim VAT on an invoice before you actually pay it.

For instance, if you bought a freezer for £1,500 + VAT (15%), you would receive an invoice for £1725 including VAT. You can claim back that £225 in your next account, even though you may not actually pay for the freezer for another six months.

To work out the VAT element in a tax inclusive price, such as with a petrol receipt, follow the following formula:

$$\frac{\text{rate of tax}}{\text{rate of tax} + 100}$$

Therefore, with VAT at 15%:

$$\frac{15}{15 + 100} = \frac{15}{115} = \frac{3}{23}$$

For example, if your VAT inclusive petrol bill came to £11.50, the VAT element would be ³⁄₂₃ of £11.50, which is £1.50. It is NOT 15% of £11.50.

Other Possible VAT Fractions:

Rate of Tax	VAT Fraction
4 per cent	¹⁄₂₆
5 per cent	¹⁄₂₁
6 per cent	¹⁄₁₈
8 per cent	²⁄₂₇
10 per cent	¹⁄₁₁
12½ per cent	¹⁄₉
15 per cent	³⁄₂₃
20 per cent	¹⁄₆
25 per cent	¹⁄₅

Food

Most human food is zero rated, despite mounting pressure from the EEC to introduce a higher rate of tax to comply with the rest of the Common Market. There are, however, many exceptions in our system, a few of which are listed below.

The following foods are all STANDARD rated:

ice cream, confectionery, chocolate biscuits, alcoholic drinks, soft drinks, crisps, salted or roasted nuts, pet food, home brewing products, medicines, medicated preparations, appetite suppressants and dietary supplements.

Easy isn't it? Or is it?

Ice cream is standard rated, but frozen mousses are zero rated.
Frozen Ice Cream Cakes are standard rated, but ordinary cream cakes are not.
Frozen yogurt on a stick is standard rated, but becomes zero when fresh in a tub.
Bars of chocolate are standard rated, but not chocolate spread, cooking chocolate, or drinking chocolate.

Toffees are standard rated, but not toffee apples.
Chocolate covered biscuits are standard rated, but not chocolate
covered cake.
Crisps are standard rated, but not savoury biscuits or pork scratchings.
Alcoholic drinks are standard rated, but not fruit preserved in alcohol.
Bicarbonate of Soda is standard rated, but not Baking Powder.
Malt Extract with Cod Liver Oil is standard rated, but plain Malt
Extract is not UNLESS it is for home brewing!
Salt is zero rated, unless it is for a non-food use such as water softening
or dishwashing purposes. (If you bought cooking salt in bulk and
placed a notice in it stating it was ideal for melting snow and ice, you
would have to charge VAT!)
Food supplies in the 'course of catering' are all standard rated.

To complicate matters even further there is a distinction between
'hot' and 'cold' food. Hot take-away foods are standard rated, and
cold foods zero rated. So, if you sell a cold pie it is zero rated. If you
heat it up in a microwave oven you will have to charge VAT. Likewise,
a toasted sandwich is standard rated, but an ordinary sandwich is zero
rated. Hot tea and coffee are standard rated, but not iced tea or coffee!

Motor Cars

You cannot reclaim VAT paid on a motor car, even if it is used wholly
for business purposes, such as for a driving school. On the other hand,
you do not have to account for VAT when selling a car which has been
used in your business, unless you sell it for more than you paid, in
which case you will have to pay VAT on the difference. You may not
include in the purchase price the cost of any accessories added at a later
stage.

If you use a car in connection with your business you may claim
back the VAT on ALL repairs and maintenance, even if the car is also
used for private motoring.

You may also treat the VAT on petrol used in connection with your
business as an input tax. Keep all receipts, work out roughly what
proportion of your total mileage is in connection with your business,
and claim back that percentage. All records relating to the sale and
purchase of motor cars in your business must be kept for at least three
years.

Definition of a Motor Car

For VAT purposes, a motor car is a vehicle which has three or more
wheels, and is either made mainly for the carriage of passengers, or has
side windows to the rear of the driver's seat.

You may claim back the VAT on the purchase of any vehicle used in
your business which has been constructed for a special purpose other

than carrying passengers, e.g. delivery vans, ice-cream vans, mobile shops, etc.

If you convert a vehicle into a motor car by adding side windows or rear passenger seats, and still use it for business purposes, you must pay VAT on the current value of the vehicle at the time of conversion, plus the cost of the conversion.

Business Entertainment
VAT on business entertainment CANNOT be reclaimed unless the entertainment is for an overseas customer (anyone who is not ordinarily resident in the UK), in which case 'the sky's the limit'. As long as the primary purpose is to promote your goods or services you may reclaim any VAT on meals, drinks, accommodation, theatre visits, nightclubs, and sporting and recreational facilities. And if you have enough money you can even claim on a few inexpensive items such as yachts, power boats, and private aircraft!

What is far more important for the shopkeeper is the fact that you can also reclaim VAT on any entertainment which is provided SOLELY for your employees, such as an annual outing or staff Christmas party.

Retail Schemes
To help your accounting procedures there are nine BASIC VAT Retail Schemes to choose from, and each is described fully in separate leaflets. The following is a brief description of each:

SCHEME	CONDITIONS	HOW IT WORKS
A	Cannot be used if you have zero rated sales.	To find your output tax you simply multiply your gross takings for the period by the VAT fraction.

THE FOLLOWING SCHEMES CAN BE USED WHERE THERE ARE SUPPLIES AT BOTH STANDARD AND ZERO RATES.

B	Your takings from zero rated sales must not exceed 50% of your turnover in a year.	Record the expected selling prices of zero rated goods you have received and then take this away from your daily gross takings to find your standard rated takings, then multiply by the VAT fraction.
(B1)	No 50% turnover limit from zero rated goods.	Works in the same way as Scheme B, but you will have to make an annual stock adjustment.

(B2)	Your turnover has to be less than £500,000 a year.	You have to apply fixed mark-ups according to the type of zero rated goods involved. Take this total away from your gross takings to find your standard rated takings and multiply by VAT fraction.
C	You have to have a turnover of less than £90,000 per year.	Add up the cost of all standard rated goods you have received, including VAT, and add on a statutory mark-up according to your trade, then multiply by the VAT fraction. Examples of mark-up are as follows: News con tob 16⅔%, Grocers, Butchers, Bakers 20%, Greengrocers, Electrical Goods, Bookshops, Chemists 40%, Health Food Shops 50%, Jewellers 75%.
D	You have to have a turnover of £500,000 a year or less.	You work out the ratio of zero rated to standard rated purchases, and apply this to your gross takings, then calculate output tax accordingly. Once a year you make an annual adjustment.
E	You have to be able to work out your standard rated stock on hand when you start the scheme.	You work out the expected selling prices of both your stock and standard rated goods received during the period, and calculate the amount of VAT due on the total accordingly.
(E1)	You have to be able to work out opening and closing stocks of standard rated lines only.	You work out the sales of each 'line' of goods which has the same selling price, and then add them together. Then multiply by the VAT fraction.
F	You must be able to separate your takings at the till.	Add up standard rated sales for the period and multiply by VAT fraction.
G	There are no limits to this scheme.	Scheme G is very similar to Scheme D, apart from the fact that you have to add one eighth to the resulting output Tax.

H	You need to work out your stock on hand when you start the scheme.	You have to r selling prices including V/ period, and between st< goods. This is u... your gross takings, and VAт calculated on the standard rated portion.
J	As for 'H'	Scheme J is similar to Scheme H except that it is based on your trade over a full year. At the end of each year you compare your calculations with what you have actually sold and make an 'annual adjustment'.

If your business is closed down, or sold, or the trading style alters, you must notify your local VAT office in writing within ten days of the change.

VAT Rates Through The Years
1 April 1973   Standard rate introduced @ 10%
29 July 1974   Standard rate reduced to 8%
18 Nov 1974   Higher rate introduced @ 25%
12 April 1976   Higher rate reduced to 12½%
18 June 1979   Higher rate abolished, and standard rate raised to 15%

Leasing a business

Although the lease is often placed far in the background by the average prospective purchaser, who is more concerned with location, turnover, gross profits, competition, etc., the lease is one of the most important factors in your purchase. It is, in fact, the rules and regulations governing your stay in the premises, and must be thoroughly vetted by your solicitor before signing any document, because it is usually written in such a manner as to make it practically incomprehensible to the layman.

This section is written to provide you with a general synopsis of a typical lease, in plain English, so that you may understand what is involved. It is not meant to replace your solicitor.

The lease will generally commence by stating the name and address of the landlord, the name and address of the tenant, and the date on which the lease was signed. It will then proceed to identify the property, called the 'demised premises', with a coloured outline on an ached plan. After this will come the date of the commencement of the lease, and the period of years. Then will come the amount of rent payable, and when it should be paid. This will usually be on one of the normal quarter days (25 March, 24 June, 29 September, 25 December), and will be payable in advance. Note should also be taken of any set rent review periods, and the date when the next rent review occurs, as this may substantially decrease your profits.

The length of lease given tends to become shorter as time progresses. In the 'good old days', leases were usually given for 21 years or more, with rent reviews every seven years. I remember one shop I purchase in 1965 had 20 years to run on the lease, with no revisions, at £150 *per annum*. That meant that the rent on that shop would still only be £3 per week in 1985! Nowadays, this type of lease has been superseded by the 15 year lease with five-year reviews, although many leases have been agreed for 12 years, nine years, seven years, and even less, with two- or three-year revisions. A point to bear in mind, is that the longer the period between reviews, the more the rent will increase at such time. In the case of my old shop quoted above, I have no doubt that the new rent in 1985 would have increased to at least £3,000 per annum.

The lease will then state the procedure for negotiating a new rent at each of the reviews, including what will happen if an agreeable figure cannot be reached. Any revision should be at the current market value, but there will almost certainly be a clause limiting any new rental figure to be at least that of the old one. In other words, the rent can never go down.

After this will probably come a list of covenants which the lessee has to conform to. For example:

(1) To pay the full amount of rent on the agreed dates.
(2) To pay all existing and future rates, taxes, and other outgoings, whether local or parliamentary.
(3) To pay the building insurance premiums against loss or damage by fire, lightning, explosion and aircraft. This may be arranged by the lessee, or through the landlord at the lessee's expense.
(4) To keep the premises clean, and in a good state of repair.
(5) If the lease is a full repairing one, as most are, to paint the outside of the property every three years, and to paint the inside every five years. And on the occasion the outside is painted, also to varnish or colour whatever else had previously been so dealt with, and on the occasion of internal painting, also to varnish and colour all parts that had been so dealt with, and to paper with suitable paper any parts that had been previously papered.
(6) To comply with all statutory requirements from any local or public authority, e.g. Health & Safety at Work etc. Act 1974, and

the Offices, Shops and Railway Premises Act 1963.

(7) To execute within three months any repairs required by the landlord for which the lessee is liable.

(8) To permit the landlord, or his representatives, to enter and take inventories and view the state of repair, at reasonable hours in the daytime.

(9) Not to use the premises for any other purpose than that mentioned in the lease without the landlord's consent. This clause may also mention various items that must not be stored on the premises, such as petroleum or other inflammable spirit.

(10) Not to hold auctions.

(11) Not to permit a nuisance or annoyance to the neighbours.

(12) Not to make any alterations to the building without the written consent of the landlord.

(13) Not to do anything on the premises which may prejudice the building's insurance.

(14) Not to assign or sublet any part of the property without the written consent of the landlord, which will not be unreasonably withheld.

(15) In the event of the lessee not wishing to renew the lease at its expiration, to permit the landlord to affix a notice board to a suitable part of the premises, for reletting.

(16) To inform the landlord, and take any necessary steps to prevent any encroachments on the property.

(17) At the end of the lease, or sooner, to yield up the premises and fixtures and fittings duly repaired, painted and maintained.

After all these undertakings on the part of the lessee, the landlord then undertakes to allow the lessee to 'peaceably and quietly hold and enjoy the demised premises during the said term without any lawful interruption' as long as the lessee complies with his covenants.

If the name of the vendor is not on the lease, it means that it has changed hands at least once since it was created, and that there must be an Assignment of the Lease in existence.

The question that occurs most frequently to newcomers to business is 'What happens when the lease ends? Do we lose everything?' The brief answer is as follows:

The tenant does have a degree of legal protection under the law on the termination of his lease, but not as much as a tenant in a residential property. Subject to certain conditions, the tenant must be offered a new lease on similar terms to the old one, although the rent will now be the current market rent. The duration of the lease must be reasonable compared with the original.

In practice, what generally happens is that the landlord's surveyor will suggest a rental figure far in excess of that at which he hopes to settle. You now have two choices, either to negotiate direct with the surveyor yourself, or to instruct your own surveyor to act on your behalf. I have done both, and am personally in favour of the former, having obtained just as good, if not better, results from my own efforts. The procedure is very simple. First, measure the square footage of the sales area of your shop, and then contact a local estate agent to find out the going rate per square foot in your locality. This price will be for the first 20 foot at the front of your shop. If your shop is much deeper, assess it at a slightly lower figure. Multiply the two amounts (square footage × price per square foot), and add on a figure for the accommodation, if any. This will give you a fair rental figure. Compare this to the rents of your neighbouring shops, bearing in mind when their rents were fixed, and you should end up with a pretty accurate idea of what the rent should be. You then offer a lower figure than this to the surveyor together with a letter setting out details of how the shopping parade has deteriorated in the past couple of years, and all your other hard luck stories. If he insists on the original rental figure, suggest it goes to arbitration. In almost all cases a satisfactory compromise will be reached.

The advantages of negotiating for yourself are that you will know that all letters are being answered immediately, and that you will save on surveyor's fees. If you employ a Chartered Surveyor to act for you in negotiations, you can expect his fee to be about 7 1/2 per cent of the rent agreed. It is possible however, in some instances, to agree a rough figure initially, based on the amount of work anticipated.

Perhaps I have been unlucky with my choice of surveyors, but I shall now give two actual examples of rent negotiations that have happened to me in the last few years.

Examples of Rent Negotiations

(1) New Lease: Local Surveyor Acting on my Behalf My lease was for 15 years, with five year revisions, at £900 per annum. Six months before it expired, my solicitor applied for a new lease, and we were offered a new one for a period of 12 years, with three-year revisions, at £3,000 per annum. I was advised to contact a local surveyor to negotiate on my behalf, and engaged one recommended by my bank manager. He spent an hour or so making notes, and then told me a fair rent would be in the region of £2,400 per annum. On my suggestion he offered £1,600. Letters passed very slowly between various parties for well over a year, until eventually my surveyor reported back saying that the best he could do was £2,200 per annum, and advised me to accept it. I refused, and told my solicitor to inform the landlord that I wished to go to arbitration. A couple of weeks later the landlord's surveyor arrived in the shop with a new proposal of £2,000. I said I would agree this figure if the lease were amended to 15 years with five-year revisions. This was accepted.

(2) Rent Review: Personally Negotiated The lease was again for 15 years, with five-year revisions, at £1,375 per annum. At the review we were asked to agree a new rental figure of £4,600. We offered £1,800, and soon settled at £2,600 per annum.

Exceptions to granting a new lease

Coming back to the conditions referred to earlier under which a landlord need not grant a new lease, the exceptions are:

(a) If there has been a serious breach of the repair convenant. The operative word here is 'serious'. A list of minor repairs not completed, or a particular year when the outside should have been painted and was not, would not constitute a serious breach.
(b) Persistent long delays in paying the rent.
(c) Any other serious breach of a covenant. However, it must be really serious, such as using the premises for illegal purposes.
(d) If the landlord is able to offer alternative comparable premises in the area, on similar terms.
(e) If the lessee is only occupying part of the premises, with the rest being vacant, it may be possible to allow the landlord to be able to offer the premises as a whole.
(f) If the landlord wishes to demolish the premises for redevelopment and actually does.
(g) If the landlord wishes to occupy the premises for his own use, and actually does, as long as he has held an interest in the property for at least five years.

The landlord must give six months notice, and state whether he is prepared to give a new lease or not.

If you have reason not to believe a landlord if he states that he wishes to repossess the property in order to occupy it or redevelop it, you are entitled to apply to the county court for a judgment, and unless the landlord can prove his intentions, the court is bound to order an extension to the lease. Compensation is calculated as being two-and-a-quarter times the rateable value of the shop. Unless the tenant or his predecessors in business have been in occupation for 14 years or more, when it is four-and-a-half times the rateable value.

Immediately you receive notice, give it to your solicitor. Better still make sure your solicitor contacts the landlord's solicitor to discuss this at least six months before the expiration date of the lease.

Landlords and Landladies

Over the past many years I have owned seven different shops. Two have been freehold, one was owned by a large insurance company, one by the local council, and curiously enough, the other three were all owned by women. I call them 'The Good', 'The Bad', and 'The Ugly'.

I could write an entire book on them alone, especially 'The Ugly'; instead, I will just give a brief description of each, not that it will be of any direct benefit to you, but solely to make you aware of what you may have to contend with in the future.

'The Good'

She was the only landlady of mine that I ever actually met. She was a business woman, who also owned several other properties, and although she drove a hard bargain with negotiations, there was never any nastiness involved, and all matters were eventually amicably agreed. If ever we had any queries, perhaps regarding insurance, extending the property, or even references, she replied immediately with a definite answer. On our part, we kept the premises in good repair, and always paid our rent on time. On hers, she never bothered us. We had a peaceful eight years.

'The Bad'

She was the first landlady I had. She had run the shop herself previously for many years, and completely neglected to keep it in a reasonable condition. She had sold it on lease to the vendors from whom we were buying, and I suppose was too ashamed to mention to them the repairs that were needed. However, when our turn came to sell, she sent along a surveyor, and then came down like a ton of bricks on every minor flaw he found, disregarding the fact that in the previous two years we had improved the property tremendously.

Two incidents regarding the repairs stick in my memory. The first was when the surveyor wanted part of the kitchen repainted. Having already repainted most of the property, we had several part-filled tins left, and made up a most obnoxious colour by mixing them all together, and used this on the kitchen walls. The expression on the surveyor's face when he came to re-inspect was a picture.

The other incident concerned the shop floor. The surveyor said it had a slight 'springiness' in one part and we should have the joists looked at to remedy this. Not only was the floor tiled, but it would also have involved removing half the shop to get at the boards. This was obviously impossible. I removed a couple of floorboards from under the stairs, and slid underneath the floor, wedging the offending joist in place with a sweet jar. (They were made of glass in those days). Fortunately it stood up to the surveyor bouncing on the spot, and after a few more visits from him, she granted the Licence to Assign. On the day we moved out, she asked us if we would like to buy the freehold!

When we received our final bank statements we saw that the bank had not followed our instructions, and was still paying the rent. And she was still accepting it!

'The Ugly'

She had served a Schedule of Dilapidations on the vendor, eight pages long. To be fair, the property had only been lived in occasionally over the years by successive owners, and was in a poor state of repair. The vendor had always been in arrears with his rent, and had no money to pay for the necessary repairs. To solve the problem, I suggested that we withhold £5,000 from the purchase price, and if the vendor did not effect the repairs within six months, we would use the money to comply with the Schedule. This was agreed to by all parties, and the Licence to Assign was duly issued.

Six months later the landlady asked if the repairs had been effected, and when told that they had not, and that I was enclosing details of estimates I had received from two builders for doing the necessary work, she replied that she was not interested in any private agreement made between the vendor and myself, and that as the work had not been completed within six months, she was now going to take steps to make us forfeit the lease. Our solicitor eventually straightened her out on this, and the next two years were spent having similar confrontations over minor incidents. It even took us almost a year before receiving payment of an insurance claim made through her on the shop ceiling, and which she hung on to, obviously hoping we had forgotten. It was a lovely feeling when everything was completed, and we knew we would never have any contact with her again.

Contracts

Clause of Restraint of Trade

Unless one of these clauses is incorporated into the contract, there could be the most serious consequences for the purchaser. Imagine your reaction and the loss of trade if, after buying a shop, you suddenly find the vendor is about to open another shop in the same trade, a few doors away. Fortunately, this can be avoided for a time anyway, by a Restraint of Trade Clause, which prohibits the vendor from operating a shop in a similar trade within a certain distance for a set period of time, such as within three miles for two years. You will not be able to stop him working in the same trade for all time, or at an unreasonable distance, but you should have become sufficiently well established by the end of the Restraint not to have any problems in the event of him wishing to compete. Some sort of insight into the vendor's intentions may be gleaned from his reaction to your solicitor's initial suggestion on time and distance.

PART 3

Now You're In Business . . .

To Begin With

My advice for your first few weeks in the shop is to alter nothing. Buy from the same suppliers, maintain the same pricing structure, keep the same staff, and open the same hours. This way you should earn the same profit. These weeks will soon pass, and should be spent monitoring the trade generally, formulating your own policies, and getting ready for your change of ownership 'display'. Take note of when most people pass the shop, because you may find that you can increase your takings by altering your opening hours, without extending them. As an example of this, I once bought a grocer's shop on the edge of an industrial estate which was open all day Saturday, and closed on Wednesday afternoons. After a couple of weeks I soon realised that Saturday afternoons were a dead loss, as most of the trade came from the factories, and changed the half day to Saturday instead. It took quite a few weeks before people realised we were open on Wednesday afternoons, but the takings from these soon overtook those on a Saturday, and gave us the benefits of a long weekend and higher weekly takings without increasing our total hours worked.

Another case comes to mind of someone who noticed a potential trade around seven o'clock in the evening, whilst his morning takings were minimal. He changed his hours to opening from ten o'clock in the morning until eight o'clock at night, and was very pleased with the result. Especially as he never liked getting up in the morning anyway.

I believe you should try to change the appearance of the shop from the outside in some manner, to encourage new customers into the shop. If you do not present a difference to the public from the outside, those members of the public who have not been into the shop for some time will not even realise it has changed hands. Your main priority is to encourage the public through the door. However, if you do this immediately, on the first day or two, without improving the inside, you may not succeed in keeping them if they were not satisfied before. You have to encourage them in, and then offer them something better, cleaner, cheaper, or more efficient than before. Perhaps it is rather drastic, but I know of one person who, when he buys a shop, closes it for two weeks whilst he completely alters the inside to his own design, to make the greatest impact. He swears by this method. Personally, I think this is unnecessary because it does not allow you to take into account the profitable parts of the business which have been built up over the years. But it does show the importance some people place on presenting a different image to the public.

Making Changes: Fittings and Equipment

Fittings

Have a good look at the following areas of your shop, and see where improvements can be made:

(1) Shop Fronts First impressions count! This expression may be hackneyed, but it is true. The first impression your shop presents to a potential customer is obtained from your shopfront. It is amazing how much difference a coat of paint can make. Keeping the shopfront clean and bright is probably one of the cheapest and best methods of advertising, but can easily be neglected as shopkeepers tend not to look at their own shops from the outside. If the woodwork is showing signs of deterioration, you have several choices:

(a) You can have the old rotten wood cut out and replaced. This is the cheapest method, and not necessarily the worst.

(b) You can have a new metal shopfront. This of course, is much more expensive, but has the advantage of possibly giving more sales area in the shop, plus a choice of having the doorway enlarged, or positioned differently. Planning permission will be necessary, but is usually arranged by the replacement window company.

(c) You can have a completely new window made up by a specialist firm or local craftsman, from hardwood. Prices vary, and advantages are similar to (b).

(d) You can have the existing glass, wooden frame, and door replaced only. Local carpenters will be able to quote for this, and planning permission will not be necessary.

(2) Fascias Just as important as the shopfront, is the fascia. This should be eye-catching, and the wording kept as simple as possible. It may be hand-painted, or perspex, or illuminated, or made up of stuck-on letters. If you are a member of a group, you may be able to get some financial assistance towards replacing yours, and if you do not mind products being advertised one or two firms may even put one up free of charge. The most obvious people to contact are the tobacco firms.

(3) Sunblinds These need regular attention as you will be liable for any damage or injury that may be caused by them. Try not to roll them up when they are wet.

(4) Windows Open windows will let in more light, but are not suitable for the display of valuable goods. The outsides of the windows should be cleaned regularly every week, and the insides less frequently, but sufficiently often to ensure they remain perfectly clean, and encourage the public to look at the shop. This task will be simpler if there is easy access to the window space. If you stick posters on the window, make sure all the pieces of sellotape, etc., are removed before the new posters are stuck on. A razor blade and methylated spirits, will take care of almost anything. If you have an actual window display, get into a pattern of changing it at regular intervals, at least every three weeks, so as to maintain the public's interest and save the goods from getting dusty and fading in the sunlight. Remember, a window display can be a hindrance to custom as well as an asset, if the windows are dirty and the display soiled. Because of this, and the fact that the sales area inside the shop is now considered to be more important, more and more people are discarding the conventional window area, and using the actual shop as a 'window display', particularly when they have a new shop front put in. The cost of these have come down over recent years, and they are quick and easy to install, as well as making the shop more modern and clean-cut in appearance.

(5) Floors Possibly the most striking thing about a shop once you have entered it, is the floor. Just as a new fitted carpet can completely alter the visual impact of a room, so can the condition of your lino or tiles set the tone of your shop.

   If your floor is worn out in places and you cannot afford to have it all renewed, then make sure you repair the parts that are unsightly. If you cannot do it yourself ask a flooring firm to have a look and make some suggestions. Once the floor is in good condition — show it off. Do not leave it cluttered, so that customers may trip. Sweep it at least once a day, and wash it as frequently as necessary. A weekly buff with an electric polisher also works wonders.

(6) Lighting Adequate lighting is essential in the main shop area, and can enhance the wall shelving displays when strategically placed. Fluorescent tubes gradually grow dimmer over a period of time, imperceptibly maybe, but dimmer all the same. This is why some shops make a practice of changing all the tubes at set intervals, rather than waiting for them to burn out. Fluorescent tubes come in various shades, and the correct colour should be used for each application.

(7) Shelving You can give the impression of having new shelving, simply by replacing the front plastic edging strips in a bright new

colour. After all, when the shelves are filled, this is the only part the customer can see!

(8) Ceiling and Walls A coat of emulsion paint on the ceiling and walls, and gloss paint where necessary, will complete the transformation of the shop interior, at minimal cost. These do not need painting very often, and because of this are very often neglected simply because they are not noticed.

(9) Electrics If you have any electrical work carried out in the shop or above, it would be beneficial to have extra power points placed strategically in the shop area and/or stockroom. You cannot have too many, and you never know when you may need them.

(10) Telephones If you live above the premises, or use part of it as an office or stock room, and do not have an intercom system, it is well worth while having a proper press button one installed by British Telecom in place of your present system.

Equipment

The basic equipment needed for the majority of shops is a cash register, a check-out or counter on which to place it, and various types of shelving for the walls and gondolas. Most service industries require specialist equipment, e.g. launderettes, dry cleaners, etc., but apart from this type of shop, the most expensive equipment is used in the food trade, whether by a delicatessen, an ordinary grocer, a butcher, or a fast food takeaway. There are scales, fridges, freezers, cold rooms, meat slicers, vacuum packers, mincers, ovens, bains-maries, fryers, hot cabinets, extractor fans, tables, chairs, crockery and cutlery. And much, much more.

With most of these you have a choice of buying outright, leasing, or hire purchase.

Buying Outright If you have the cash to spare, you will be better off buying outright. If not, approach you 'friendly' bank manager to see if he is willing to grant a loan, and if so, on what terms. Then compare all the figures, and decide.

Hire Purchase Is literally what it says. You hire the equipment, usually over three years, and then purchase it with a final payment. Although the interest may be set against tax, it is an expensive method of borrowing. You will of course, be able to claim for capital allowances.

Leasing Leasing can usually be arranged on most items of equipment, and again is not cheap. You pay a rent for a set period of years, the whole of which is tax deductible. After the agreed number of years, a yearly peppercorn rent is usually agreed upon, which may actually never be collected. Officially, you never become the owner of the equipment. If you want to own the piece of equipment — choose hire purchase.

Hire Purchase or Leasing Agreements It has often been said that no one should sign a contract of any sort without reading and clearly understanding *all* the 'small print', and if necessary having a solicitor giving it a 'once-over'. Regardless of this advice, although everyone knows it to be true, most hire purchase and leasing agreements are signed on the spot by owners of small businesses, with just a cursory glance over the deliberately complicated wording on the back. This can prove very costly if you wish to settle early, or if something goes wrong with the equipment. It will also tell you, if you look very closely, who will be the eventual owner of the equipment.

An example of this was the case of the grocer who was told by a rep that he could buy a till, and pay for it over five years. He understood he was also receiving a five-year repair and maintenance contract. At the end of the year he was asked to pay for a service contract for the rest of the time, as the guarantee was for the first year only. When he questioned this he also found out that he was not actually buying the machine, but only hiring it for five years. He obviously signed an agreement without reading it.

Guarantees on Equipment When placing orders for equipment, new or secondhand, on which a guarantee is offered, make sure the equipment is guaranteed from the date of *delivery*, not from the *order* date. It could happen that you only end up with a three-month guarantee instead of one for six months, if there is a three-month delay for some reason on delivery!

Some manufacturers and installers allow a period of three days after delivery of a piece of equipment to report any faults. If you do not inform the company within this time you will have no claim on them for parts not covered by the guarantee.

Disputes If you have a dispute involving a sum of money less than £500, and do not wish to get involved with solicitor's costs, you should consider making use of the 'small claims' procedure. A booklet called *Small Claims in the County Court* is available from the court, and free impartial advice can be obtained from the Citizen's Advice Bureau.

Regarding the choice of equipment, do not squander your money on anything which is unnecessary, nor choose a piece of equipment which is much larger or of far better quality than you need. There is no direct comparison between the money spent on an item and the sales it generates. For instance take an item such as a dairy cabinet, which is used in many trades. If you take £200 per week from a four-foot cabinet costing £1,300, you are unlikely to take any more if you £2,000 on the same-sized cabinet. Likewise, depending on your of trade of course, you will not double your weekly turnover by buying two cabinets for £2,600. If you did this, you should also remember that you will lose out on possibly 20 feet of ordinary shelving, plus extra electricity costs.

If you are thinking of buying secondhand equipment, ensure that all necessary parts are included and that no part appears excessively worn. If this is the case, enquire as to the cost of fitting a new part before buying, because you could find yourself spending far more than you bargained for.

This happened to me fairly recently when I bought an X-Firm's bacon slicer from a store which was closing down. The machine was one of the recent grey and stainless steel type, was in excellent condition, and at a virtual giveaway price. I noticed that one of the grinding wheels was broken, but thought that would not cost much to replace.

I did not use the machine for some time, and when I finally decided to bring it into service I noticed that the apparently perfect blade had a small bite out of it. I knew these were expensive, but if properly looked after, should last for years. It was then that it struck me — there was no 'gate' with the machine. The gate is a piece of metal approximately 12" × 5" which clips onto the moving bed and incorporates a series of hooks which are activated by a lever to hold the meat firm whilst cutting.

The people I bought the machine from could not find the original gate, and so I contacted X-Firm to order a new blade, a new grinding wheel, a new gate, and asked for the machine to be serviced. This was duly done, and I was very proud of my gleaming new machine. Imagine my horror when I received a bill from X-Firm demanding the sum of £383.61.

I scanned through the invoice and was astounded to see that the gate was priced at £180. I immediately telephoned X-Firm, respectfully pointing out that they must have made a mistake.

'No,' they informed me, 'that is our price.'

'I cannot see how you can possibly justify charging £180 for a 12" × 5" piece of metal', I replied, thinking to myself that I could have bought a television or a washing machine for that price.

The man from X-Firm was indignant. 'The gate is not just a piece of metal. It is a very complex high precision piece of machinery and is only made in very small quantities for machines such as yours which are old and obsolete.'

I stared at the gate in a new light. It looked exactly the same as all the other gates I had seen adorning various models both old and new, for years. Eventually, after many letters had been sent back and forth, and they had shown no signs of reducing the figure asked for, I paid up.

I had learnt another lesson the hard way.

The following couple of items of equipment are found in all types of shops, and a few words about them may not come amiss.

Cash registers Great advances have been made in the last few years with the advent of microchips, and the new cash registers are now very sophisticated, and most reasonably priced. In fact, if all you need is a simple till, they are cheaper now than they have ever been. The ones with different departments though, prove more useful and informative, allowing you to isolate any sector of your trade.

When buying an electronic till, satisfy yourself that in the event of anything going wrong with it, you will be able to have it repaired promptly. It is no use having to wait for two days for a mechanic to come out, who knows little more than you do, and who then takes the machine away to 'test on the bench' for two weeks.

This happened to us a few years ago. Our local cash and carry was selling a certain make of electronic till at a very special price, and we took advantage of this and bought two of them. A few months later, whilst still under guarantee, one of the tills stopped printing, and we telephoned the London address on the guarantee card, and were informed that the line was no longer in existence. A long-distance telephone call to the importers up North followed, and we were told that they were having a little trouble with servicing, but they would get someone down to me as soon as possible. Five days later a mechanic turned up from Crawley, could not mend the till, and took it away for three weeks, explaining when it was returned, that they had to wait for a spare part to be sent from . . . ?

Two weeks later I received a bill for £85 from the Crawley firm for the repair. Needless to say I did not pay it, but I could have done without all the telephone calls and letters and hassle that followed. You have been warned. If you have electronic tills I suggest you keep your eyes open for a good cheap second-hand electric or manual till to keep as reserve for emergencies. I can assure you, in the long run it will not cost you any money. Whilst on the subject of cash registers, it is best if they are sited so that the amounts and total can be seen by the customer, to minimise any dishonesty by the staff.

Floats A 'float', for the uninitiated, is the total amount of all the loose change in the till at the start of the day. This figure is then deducted from the total amount of cash, cheques, bills, etc., at the end of the day, and should agree with the takings registered. My method, when checking the till at the end of the day, is to total all the loose change first, and make a note of this on a separate piece of paper. This forms the float for the following day. With regard to takings, it is much easier

if amounts in multiples of £1 only are entered into the cash book, and
the remaining odd pence deducted from the following day's float, and
rung up separately as the first cash sale. As a reminder of this, I always
kept the relevant piece of paper in the cash drawer. The illustration
below will show more clearly what I mean.

Loose change	14.92		14.92
Total of notes etc.	465.00	Amount to ring up	.78
	479.92	New float	14.14
Less: previous	13.14		
day's float			
Takings for the day	466.78		

Takings entered in cash book as £466.00

How to use a calculator From my experience, strange as it may seem,
most people do not know how to use a calculator. They make no use
of the decimal point, and then have to guess at the resultant figure.
This is all right if you are multiplying the same type of numbers all the
time, but can lead to serious errors if you use it for anything more
complicated. If you are not conversant with the proper way to use a
calculator, study the following: One pound is 1.00, ten pence is .10,
one penny is .01, a halfpenny (may not be physically used, but useful
to know all the same) is .005. Therefore one pound sixty seven and a
half pence is 1.675, ten pounds and threepence is 10.03.

Petty Cash Box Whether you employ staff or not, I think it is a good
idea to have a petty cash box. The main reason for this is that it is all
too easy to pay out for items such as milk, cleaning materials,
Sellotape, etc., and then forget, and not enter them into the cash book,
for setting off against tax. If you pay for odd items from the till, even if
you have a 'paid out' key, it is not always possible to remember
everything at the end of the day, and by the end of the year these can
amount to a sizeable sum of money.

The second reason is that it is best, in my view, to keep the cash
register for that purpose, i.e. to register the amount of cash taken, and
not to be opened willy-nilly. It is an added security measure.

The method recommended is first to find or purchase a suitable box,
then decide how much of a float will be sufficient for the week, and
then place that amount in the box, together with a pad of petty cash
vouchers, which may be purchased from most stationers.

The procedure for making payments is very simple. Every time cash
is taken from the box a petty cash voucher should be made out
showing a description of the goods, the cost, and the signature of the
person making the payment, together with a receipt where possible.

Checking the petty cash is simply a matter of totalling the cash and all the vouchers, and ensuring they match your original float. For most shops, a float of £20 should suffice.

Equipment: do you need it? When faced with the choice of buying a piece of equipment or not, ask yourself the following question.

'Will it save time, and if so, will that time saved be able to be put to profitable use, or will it just mean that the existing staff will have nothing to do for an additional period of the day?'

Shop Layout

Watch for bottlenecks, and how the general layout of the shop may be altered for the better. Make a scale plan, and move counters and equipment around. If you are thinking of replacing the shopfront, take this opportunity of reappraising the whole shop and if necessary calling in several shopfitting firms for their opinions.

As each shop is different it is impossible to be specific about layout. The following points should however be borne in mind.

(1) The customer should be made to shop the whole store. This is most easily done, if you are using central gondolas, by ensuring that there are odd numbers of them. It does not matter about the quantity. See illustration below:

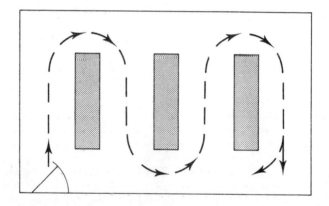

(2) There are two schools of thought regarding the height of central gondolas. Some people say they should not be too tall, for security reasons. Others say that this is nonsense, because if you can see the customer, he can see you, and no matter how low the gondola is, you will never be able to see what he is doing with his hands. The only indisputable fact is that with tall gondolas you can display more stock.

(3) Aisles should be sufficiently wide to allow one person to look at

the display, and another to walk by easily.
(4) One door, or two separate ones? There are pros and cons fo
  depending on the situation. But bear in mind that security is
  easier with one door.
(5) Try to arrange the shop so that all areas are supervised.

Displaying Stock

(1) Try to group the same products together, and relate them to ones
  on either side.
(2) Display vertically, not horizontally, e.g.

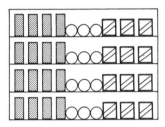 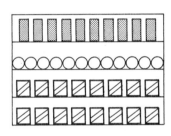

(3) Merchandise the shelves frequently by bringing forward the goods
  on the shelves, keeping them dusted, and not allowing them to
  become hidden behind others.

Security

There has been a tremendous escalation in the number of burglaries in
recent years, and no type of trade appears to be less vulnerable than
another. Even offices, dentists', estate agents', and the like are broken
into, presumably in the hope of finding some petty cash on the
premises. It is only common sense to ensure your premises are as
secure as possible, within both reason and financial limits.

Doors Should be bolted whenever possible, and any locks used should
be of the five lever deadlock mortice type. On no account rely on
cheap, or Yale-type locks, as these can be opened with the minimum of
effort.

Windows Should have proper locks fitted, or bars, and should not be
left with just a catch which can easily be undone by smashing the glass.
Any windows which are not used should be screwed down or rendered
ineffective with coachbolts, or even, as in the case of a bank I know,
welded together.

Skylights Are a favourite means of entry, and carry the same comments
as 'windows'.

Shop Windows In the past, metal grilles or steel shutters were only used by jewellers, furriers, and other shops with very high value stocks. Nowadays they are far more common amongst all trades, and prevent a certain amount of vandalism.

Protection of these vital areas, doors, windows, and skylights, may still not be enough. One reads in the newspaper occasionally of instances like a grocer losing a couple of thousand pounds worth of wines and spirits, when thieves gained entry by drilling a hole through an outside wall.

Burglar Alarms Manufacturers of these have made giant strides forward in recent years, and their systems are now very sophisticated, and actually cheaper in many instances than they were a few years ago. They are generally activated by movement, body heat, vibration, or noise, and many have the advantage of minimal installation costs, because they do not need the elaborate wiring up required by the original systems. If you want more protection, a complete system using a combination of one or more of these sensors, plus pressure pads and various wired circuits is recommended.

The control box is usually sited in an accessible position, and will probably have a timed delay on it, to allow time to enter and deactivate the alarm, or leave without it ringing immediately. An alarm box is mounted outside the shop, and is a deterrent to the spur of the moment thief. Another box can be placed at the rear of the shop, or alternatively, a dummy one displayed there. Almost all systems are run on batteries, or a combination of mains and batteries, and are automatically activated if tampered with.

Apart from the initial installation costs there will be an annual maintenance charge. You can of course, fit one yourself or get a friend to fit it for you, but make sure your insurance company accepts this. Insurance companies have vested interests in various alarm companies, and usually insist you use one of those.

Handling cash Money is a problem. Everyone tries to take as much of it in the shop as possible, yet the more we take, the more problems we have in getting it to the bank. Cash should be banked regularly, not only to keep your balance as high as possible, but also, just as importantly, to reduce the risk of loss from burglary in the shop, or being attacked on the way to the bank. Insurance companies will usually only insure cash on the premises and on the way to the bank, up to a certain limit, which is not very high, so it makes sense to keep as little as possible on the premises. When going to the bank it is advisable to vary your days and times as much as possible, so that your movements are not predictable. It can be very useful having someone accompany you, especially to explain to traffic wardens if you happen to park on a yellow line. However, this is not always possible, and creates problems if your bank is a distance away. Of course, if you are lucky enough to have a bank on the same parade, your problems are solved.

One way of minimising the risks is to make use of the Post Office National Girobank facility if you have a post office nearby. All you have to do is open an account, and then pay in your cash as often as you wish — twice daily if need be. If you do not wish to get rid of your ordinary bank account you could use the post office as a paying-in station, and then pay a Girobank cheque in to your ordinary bank account once or twice a week, and thus not have to carry cash, and also alleviate any bank charges you would have had by paying in the same.

Another way of minimising risks is to use the night safe facilities of your bank. On payment of an annual fee, usually paid in quarterly instalments, you are issued with a night safe pouch and a key to the night safe outside the bank. You are then free to use the safe as many times as you wish, at any time of the day or night, and will find it most useful at weekends and holiday times when the bank is closed. For the small amount of extra money involved, I consider it well worthwhile to have two pouches, and not to have to rely on getting back to the bank the following day to pick up the deposited one.

If you must keep cash on the premises, you would be well advised to invest in a reliable safe, and have it bolted to the floor, or set in concrete, or permanently fixed by some other means. Your insurance company will advise you on makes of safe.

Do not make up wages or handle cash in view of the public. This is asking for trouble. Needless to say, you should remove any excess cash from the tills on a regular basis, in order to reduce temptation from *any* quarter.

Shoplifting Or, as I prefer to call it, *stealing*. Any good salesman will tell you that it is much easier to sell an article if the customer is allowed to handle it. This is the precept modern self-service stores adhere to, but is perhaps more aptly described by a saying which originated in America a few years ago — 'If they can't steal it, they won't buy it'. The problem is therefore, how to take advantage of such an increase in sales, and still keep losses to a minimum.

Counters and display shelving should be arranged in such a manner that there are no 'blind' corners where customers can stand unobtrusively and fill their pockets.

Security Mirrors These are very useful when placed in strategic positions, as is mirror-backed shelving. We had this in a newsagent's many years ago, and found that once you had worked out the various angles, and where to look, you could see virtually the whole of the shop without moving. Actually, the more mirrors there are in a shop, the better it is. It makes people conscious of the fact that they can be seen from many angles, and also makes the shop appear larger than it actually is. Have you noticed the number of mirrored pillars etc., there are in department stores such as Woolworth's, British Home Stores, and Marks and Spencer's? The drawback, apart from the initial cost, is the fact that they have to be thoroughly cleaned regularly, to look anything.

Closed Circuit Television (CCTV) Once the prerogative of the larger establishments, this is now within the reach of almost all shops due to modern technology, and may be rented at very little cost per week. Customers are now used to them, and accept them as a fact of life. It is useful if one of the cameras has a view of the checkout and the cash register display if possible.

When I installed two cameras and a monitor in my grocer's shop in 1976, I was one of the first of the small shops to do so, and was quite surprised at how well the customers accepted it. They were very interested in watching their friends on the monitor, and my percentage of profit improved immediately. Mind you, I did make a point of deliberately showing the cameras and television screen to the few customers I was suspicious of, and was most pleased when the majority of these never came into the shop again.

If cameras or other security devices are employed, notices to this effect should be prominently displayed for maximum impact.

It has been estimated that 30 per cent of all shop losses are attributable to *customers*, 40 per cent to *staff*, and the other 30 per cent to *wastage*.

Customers What type of customer should you be suspicious of? The answer is very simple — all of them. You may think I am taking a very pessimistic and fatalistic view of things, and this is not what you read in the textbooks. The trouble is, almost all textbooks are written by people who do not have any actual experience of running a shop, and although they are generally well versed in accountancy, legalities, and theories, they have not stood behind a counter looking at one of their favourite customers, and wondering if their eyes have been playing tricks on them when they thought they saw her place a packet of Brand 'x' in her large handbag, which funnily enough, she *does* always seem to have open. Believe me, one of the most suspicious of customers is 'Good old so-and-so, who comes in almost every day for a chat, and who always stays for at least half an hour, not buying very much at a time, but often retracing her steps in the shop and standing studying the shelves for ages, trying to decide what to buy. A lot of 'Good old so-and-so's' never came back into my shop again after I showed them the cameras and television. Do not believe unequivacably that your 'so and so's' are any different.

The one dead giveaway I have found over the years is, if, every time you look at a customer they are looking at you, be suspicious.

One method I have used successfully over the years when I have suspected someone of stealing, be it a customer, a member of the staff, or a delivery man, is to use what I call the 'System of Three'. Very simply, the suspect is left completely alone near the goods which you think are disappearing. After a quick check anything missing will be immediately noticeable. This is how you do a superquick stock check without using a pen, pencil or paper, and without having to remember any figures. Sounds too good to be true? Read on.

First, grab a cardboard box or self-service basket, and work your way through the shelves in question, whether they contain baked beans, batteries, cigarettes, half bottles of whisky, bars of chocolate, or whatever, and count the number of items in each facing, removing one or two packets from each line so that the number remaining is divisible by three. There is no need to remember how many there were in each line, and they should be left in a completely natural state. It takes no time at all afterwards to count each line, and if it is not a multiple of three you have got trouble. It is fair comment to say that if three items are removed you will not know. But experience says that only one or two will be taken at a time.

As prevention is better than detection, here is a list of helpful hints.

(a) Small valuable items can be protected by means of a wire threaded through some part, and connected to an alarm which sounds if the link is broken.

(b) Beware of the customers who come, in twos or threes, and whilst one person engages the salesman in conversation, their partner is left alone to steal.

(c) Watch for ticket switching. This is where the customer removes the original price tag from the goods and substitutes one at a lower price. To combat this, write a description of the goods on the tickets of larger value items, and use price tickets which split in half on the others.

(d) If you think anyone is acting suspiciously, approach them with 'Can I help you?' This will make them know they are being watched.

(e) Try to have a separate area where people can leave their bags. It might even be an idea, if you have sufficient space behind the checkout, to employ a cloakroom system whereby one half of a cloakroom ticket is stuck on the bag, and the other half given to the customer. This would save the customer having to worry about whether her bag might be stolen.

(f) If you have an office overlooking the shop, a two-way mirror would be a useful asset.

(g) If certain items are sold from separate counters and not paid for at the time of purchase, such as provisions from a separate provision counter, have them rung up on the till on a separate department, and do spot checks.

(h) Avoid leaving a display of stealable goods which cannot be supervised.

(i) Have all goods labelled or priced, to avoid leaving a customer unsupervised while you find out the price.

(j) Train staff in security procedures.

(k) When designing a new layout take particular account of security — blind corners, etc. — with regard to staff as well as customers if possible.

(l) Make sure staff are fully aware of the consequences of shoplifting, and are constantly on the lookout for it.

If you catch someone stealing The next problem is, 'What do you do if you catch someone stealing?' You have the choice of bringing a prosecution against them, which entails having to take time off to go to court and give evidence, and having the whole thing hanging over your head as well as theirs for weeks on end, with the probable outcome that the thief will appear before a sympathetic magistrate, who will take pity on their plight, and probably will not consider shoplifting as stealing anyway. You end up having a lot of hassle and gain nothing, except possibly some self-satisfaction, a reputation that you make a habit of, and enjoy prosecuting, dear little old age pensioners, and the fact that this may then deter others from trying.

The easiest way is simply to bar them from the shop. You do not have to serve anyone you do not wish to, and the matter is finished instantly. The choice is yours.

If you decide to go the whole hog and prosecute, ensure the following:

(1) Only approach the shoplifter if you are absolutely certain they have stolen something. If eventually they manage to secure a 'not guilty' verdict, you may face a hefty fine for wrongful arrest.

(2) Wait until they have left the premises before approaching them.

(3) If they refuse to return to the shop, a minimum of force may be used.

(4) Tell them in front of a witness, that you saw them steal something, and you intend to call the police.

(5) Telephone the police.

(6) Do not search the thief.

(7) Do not leave them by themselves whilst waiting for the police to arrive, and make sure they are accompanied if they wish to go to the toilet.

(8) Allow them to telephone a solicitor or friend if they wish to do so.

(9) Do not try to force an admission by threats.

(10) Follow the advice of the police after presenting them with all the facts.

The best method of keeping losses to a minimum is by having the shop adequately staffed at all times.

Security and your staff Take up references on staff before they are employed — if necessary by a telephone call. Watch out for under-ringing on the till and theft of goods or cash. Round figures e.g. £1, £5, or £10 present the biggest temptations. Look for customer/staff collusion. This usually takes the form of some goods (usually expensive items) not being rung up. Take particular note of where staff leave their shopping bags, if they bring them to work.

If you do suspect a member of staff, try to monitor all their movements surreptitiously and pay closer attention to any actions that appear excessive or out of the ordinary. For instance, there was the case of the member of staff who suddenly started paying more frequent visits to the cloakroom, and was finally detected taking an item in with her, and no trace of it afterwards. She had been concealing them on her person.

Another case involved the shopworker who suddenly offered to put out all the rubbish from the shop, and constantly cleared it round to the dustbin. One evening, a few minutes after he left work, the proprietor realised he had not asked him something and rushed round the corner to try and catch him, just in time to see the assistant retrieving some goods from one of the rubbish boxes he had hidden in the dustbin.

Wastage Wastage can be reduced by buying sensible quantities of goods, and planning ahead.

Code Words Having a code word may smack of espionage, James Bond, or children's games, but it can prove very useful in making staff aware of a particular situation, without alerting the customer. The most obvious use is when you want a customer watched who you cannot quite see from your position, or because you have to leave your position. The easiest way is to decide on a code word or a name that has no connection with anything else, and use that in a question or statement.

For example, if the code word is 'John Tompkins', it could be used in 'Have you seen John Tompkins lately?' or 'John Tompkins came in yesterday' etc. Make sure all staff are fully aware of the meaning, and are encouraged to use it whenever they have any suspicions.

Refunds I mention this now because it seems to be a particularly grey area for most customers and some shopkeepers. The fact is that you are not legally obliged to make a refund on any goods if they are not damaged or of inferior quality, i.e. if they are of 'merchantable quality', 'as described', and 'fit for their purpose'.

In other words, in the case of someone buying an article and later deciding she does not like the colour etc., or finding that she can buy the item cheaper elsewhere, you are under no obligation to make a refund. Nevertheless you can of course, if you wish to, and may find it prudent with some valued customers.

Cheques and Cheque Cards There has been a tremendous rise in cheque and credit card frauds in recent years, and to guard against this, a policy should be formulated and a set procedure be known to and carried out by all members of staff. The main points to remember are as follows:

(1) If a cheque card guarantees an amount up to £50, do not accept a cheque for a sum larger than this, on the assumption that at least the £50 will be covered. This is not so. The guarantee card covers cheques up to £50, and banks are under no obligation to honour any cheque made out for an amount over that figure, even when backed up by a cheque card.

(2) The cheque must be signed in your presence, and the signature must correspond with the one on the guarantee card. If the cheque is already signed, ask them to sign again on the back.

(3) It must have the card number written on the back by a member of staff.

(4) It must have the same code number as the card, and be dated before the expiry date shown.

(5) It is good practice to make staff write the expiry date of the card on the back of the cheque also.

(6) If you have any doubts at all about the cheque, the card, or the person — refuse to accept it.

(7) Do not change cheques for cash.

Fire Precautions

In 1981 fire brigades were called out to just under 4,300 retail premises. Of those almost a third were started by smokers' materials or electrical wiring and lighting. Nineteen per cent began with cookers. These figures are typical of most years. Eighty per cent of fires occur when shops are closed. This is one reason to have a final security walk round the shop at night.

If a few common-sense simple rules are adhered to, you will have to be extremely unlucky to suffer the consequences of fire.

(1) Discourage smoking as much as possible both by customers and staff. This is relatively simple in food shops where hygiene laws apply, but in other types of shops customers should not be

encouraged to smoke by the sight of members of staff doing so. Cigarette ends are the greatest potential source of fire, and you should also bear in mind that a great many customers dislike the smell of cigarette smoke intensely, anyway.

(2) Make sure all ashtrays and waste paper bins are emptied daily, and not left overnight.

(3) Try to ensure that all the premises, especially storage areas, are kept tidy at all times, and clear away waste cardboard.

(4) Keep rubbish away from walls outside over which cigarette ends may be thrown.

(5) Heating should not be by means of exposed electric fires.

(6) Make sure you do not have any trailing electric wires, especially near fridges and freezers. This point was brought home to us a few years ago when we returned to the shop on a Monday morning, and found ash all over the shop. It took no time to find the cause.

One of the freezers which had an automatic defrost, had somehow developed a blockage in an outlet pipe to its water collecting tray beneath, and had overflowed down the side of the freezer and on to a join in the power cable. There had obviously been a loud bang, judging by the amount of black soot up the side of the freezer, and the cable had disintegrated. We were fortunate there was nothing inflammable nearby.

(7) Have the correct type of fire extinguisher and/or fire blanket for your goods and premises handy, particularly near storage areas, and ensure all members of staff know how to use them. The drawback to most of these extinguishers, be they water, CO_2, or powder, is the weight, which is usually too heavy for a woman assistant to handle effectively. It is a good idea therefore, to keep in addition to your normal extinguisher, a small gas-filled multi-purpose one on the wall, which anyone can use, and which will deal very effectively with most small outbreaks.

Needless to say, if you are fully insured against fire, you will also have peace of mind.

In the event of a fire actually occurring which is not easily extinguishable, make sure of the following:

(a) All staff and customers are out of the building.

(b) Call the fire brigade.

(c) If you can, try to contain the fire with an extinguisher, but make sure you do not get cut off from the exit.

(d) If you cannot, close all the doors to reduce the oxygen.

(e) If at all possible, turn off the gas and electricity supplies.

Free advice on prevention may be obtained by asking your local Fire Prevention Officer to look over your premises.

Staff

Staff are a necessary evil. They have to be trained into your way of working from the start, or you may find them arriving late, standing chatting to their friends whilst customers are waiting, using your telephone for private calls, and leaving one minute before time, having already shed their overalls, donned their wellies and fur coats, and assembled all their other bits and pieces. They also have a multitude of other sins, such as being off sick, having babies, and expecting holidays.

In view of all this, plus the fact that you have to pay them, you should be certain that you need them, because nowadays (1987) the minimum you will have to pay a full-time assistant, including NI contributions, is about £92 per week. This is about £5,000 per year, and needs to be considered very carefully before making a decision to employ. In fact they are the largest single item of expense. Staff costings as a percentage of sales can vary from 5-6 per cent in the grocery trade, to about 16-17 per cent in department stores.

Having now made the decision, you must realise that the appearance and attitude of the staff is just as important as the visual aspect of the shop, because they represent the shop to the customer. The staff are capable of encouraging the casual customer to become a regular, and of driving a regular customer away for good. To create the best impression, they should be smartly dressed, their overalls cleaned regularly, and they should always greet customers with a smile. They should be told to be as helpful and obliging as possible, because by so doing, they will ensure there is sufficient profit to pay their wages. It may be very difficult at times for them to control their emotions, and follow the 'customer is always right' maxim, but it should be stressed to them that everyone's livelihood depends on keeping as many people as possible as happy as possible for as long as possible, and that if sufficient people are discouraged from entering the shop, they will be out of a job.

A point to bear in mind is that older women are *generally* more reliable and hard-working than youngsters, and it may be more beneficial to employ a couple of these part-time, rather than a school leaver full time. Do not get too friendly with staff. Try to be fair, but do not be over-generous, as this has a habit of backfiring on you by making them think you have more money than you do, and can build up a resentment that they are not receiving more wages.

Staff Management

As the face of your shop to the public will be judged by the attitudes of your staff and yourself, it is in your own interest to study how to get the best from staff, and motivate them in the best possible manner.

This is done by involving them as far as possible in the total activities of the business.

The main motivation for any worker is the wage he receives at the end of the week or month. Wages, bonuses, holidays, etc., all help to attract staff initially, and if they are sufficiently high, will keep them at work and stop them from leaving. However, increasing wages, holidays, etc., will not increase the incentive of the member of staff to work harder and thus benefit you more. These incentives will only come from *true motivators*.

True motivators The true motivators are those which recognise achievement and progress in the job, give job satisfaction, responsibility, authority, and an involvement in the business. Considerable thought should be given to the best ways of motivating individual members of staff, whilst bearing in mind the overall motivation. This will ensure the business is run in the most profitable manner. Try to make their work as interesting as possible, and keep them busy. They soon become dissatisfied if there is not enough to do, and the day starts to drag. It is a good idea to make them in sole charge of a particular job, because it gives them more of a sense of responsibility, and shows trust on your part.

Delegation Fact of life — nobody does your work as thoroughly or as well as you. If you employ staff you will have to accept this, train them to emulate you as far as possible, and then delegate whatever jobs you can. If you do not, you will be running round and round in ever-decreasing circles, whilst your staff stand there doing nothing but watch you work yourself into an early grave. Accept the fact that nothing will ever be done quite as you would do it yourself, and then you will have time to breathe, take stock and give some thought to general policies, and see where improvements can be made.

Engaging Staff

As far as wages are concerned, the more you are prepared to pay, the more applicants you will have, and therefore the larger the choice. Staff who deal with the public are representing you, and it may be necessary to pay over the odds to get the right person. Work it out this way — if you pay a crack hand an extra £10 per week, and you work on 20 per cent profit, you need to take an extra £50 per week to pay his wages. This is £10 worth of takings per day. Could that member of staff bring you an *extra* £10 or more a day? Generally, too little attention is paid to this aspect of staff usefulness.

Before advertising for or engaging staff, a job analysis should be done. You should write down *all* the duties involved, and a rough specification of the type of person you require for this job. An example is shown on page 84.

Advertising This should be done in such a way that it will be seen by as many people as possible who may be suitable for the position. Local newspapers, cards in shop windows (including your own), and the local Job Centre are the most effective.

Be geared up and prepared for any applicants.

The Interview When a person arrives for an interview be sure to greet him or her politely, and make it obvious they are expected. The interview should take place in a quiet room, if at all possible, with no interruptions or telephone calls. *Do not take too much notice of the way the applicants are dressed, unless they are particularly dirty.* If you are not used to interviewing, and feel rather nervous, just remember that however nervous you feel, the applicant will feel much worse.

Ask the applicant to fill in an Application Form for Employment. An example is shown on page 85. The Application Form is the basis of every contract of employment, and forms the background for an interview. When asking questions, start them with 'What', 'Who', 'Why', 'Where', etc., so as not to elicit simple 'yes' and 'no' answers.

JOB SPECIFICATION

JOB DESCRIPTION ....

RESPONSIBLE TO ....

RESPONSIBLE FOR ....

DUTIES INVOLVED ....

....

....

....

....

TRAINING ....

....

....

PROMOTION PROSPECTS ....

....

SALARY ....

HOURS ....

....

OVERTIME ....

HOLIDAYS ....

OTHER BENEFITS ....

....

STAFF SPECIFICATION ....

SEX ....   MARITAL STATUS ....

AGE LIMITS ....   PREFERRED AGE ....

PHYSICAL REQUIREMENTS ....

....

EDUCATION ....

....

PREVIOUS EXPERIENCE ....

PERSONAL QUALITIES ....

....

APPLICATION FORM FOR EMPLOYMENT
CONFIDENTIAL

PLEASE WRITE CLEARLY USING BLOCK LETTERS

Full Name Mr/Mrs/Miss ....

Address .... Date of Birth ....

.... Marital Status ....

.... Religion ....

Dependants .... Telephone ....

Previous Employments (last three)

Name & Address of Firm	From	To	Position	Reason for Leaving
....	....	....	....	....
....	....	....	....	....
....	....	....	....	....

Rate of Pay at Last Employment ....

Details of Education & Any Certificates

....

....

....

Interests & Hobbies

....

....

Do you Suffer from any Disability or Ill Health?

....

Date of Last Medical Examination .... Where held ....

Result of Last Medical Examination ....

Details of any Police Convictions ....

....

Do you hold a Current Driving Licence? ....

SIGNED .... DATE ....

Find out the reasons for the applicant leaving his last employment and ask if they mind you applying for a reference. A suggested format for this is shown on pages 87/88. If you are presented with a written reference in a different form, pay particular attention to what is *not* written down. As an example, a few years ago I bought a shop that was unexpectedly put on the market following the swift departure of the manager the day before stocktaking was due to be done. After a few weeks there, I had a telephone call from an irate employer, telling me what he thought of us for giving the ex-manager, whom he had subsequently employed, such a good reference. By pure chance, the past owner of the shop happened to be there at the time, and replied, 'I said he had a likeable personality, was reliable, and industrious, but I *never said anything about his honesty*'. If you have any doubt following the receipt of a reference, telephone the person in question, and ask him directly. He will probably say a lot more over the telephone than he would wish to put in writing. You can of course, telephone in the first instance rather than write, but he may be rather reticent about giving out personal opinions over the telephone to someone out of the blue.

To return to the interview, if possible give a simple test relevant to the job. Arithmetical tests can be revealing, but with modern-day technology mathematical qualities are not essential, unless of course, there is a malfunction of equipment or a power cut.

If the applicant appears suitable, explain the type of work, hours, pay, holidays, etc., by referring to your job specification chart (page 84), and find out when he can start. Try him on a month's trial, at the end of which time each party can decide if they wish to carry on working with the other.

When he starts work To start on the right footing, follow the procedure below:

(a) Tell him to start after the normal time on the first day, and greet him yourself.
(b) Show him round the place, explaining what goes on where, and introduce him to other members of the staff.
(c) Explain the job fully.
(d) Go over working conditions, pay, holidays, break times, etc. again.
(e) Find something interesting for him to do for the rest of the day.
(f) See him at the end of the day and answer any questions.
(g) Tell him what time to come in the following day, and what his duties will be.
(h) Check his progress frequently.

ANOTHER
The Corner Shop
1 High Street,
Westchester

Our ref: Personnel/PL

Your ref:

Date: 29 February 1988

B Good

The Sweetshop

New Town

Dear Sir/Madam

The applicant named overleaf has stated that he/she was employed/
is known by you as a .... from .... to ....
at a salary of ....

We would be very grateful if you could complete the attached
questionnaire and return it to us in the reply paid envelope as
quickly as possible.

Needless to say, all information supplied will be treated in the
strictest confidence.

Yours faithfully

A.N. Other (proprietor)

Wages Council

Wages Councils are independent bodies which consist of representatives of workers and employers, and independent members. They were
formed to fix statutory rates of minimum pay, holidays, and holiday
pay, and publish them in 'Wages Orders'. By law you must keep a
copy of the latest Wages Order notice on display in a position where it
can be seen by any of the employees.

Wages Inspectors work in all regions of the country, and it is their
job to see that employers pay at least the rates in the Wages Orders.
They carry out spot checks on employers' records and deal with
complaints from individual workers. If they find you have been
underpaying, they can make you pay all the back money owed up to
a period not exceeding two years, and raise the wage immediately. The

Name of Applicant .... Address ....

....

Date of Birth ....

If the applicant was employed by you please answer questions 1-14.
If not please answer questions 14-17.

1. Can you verify the dates, job description, and salary? If not
   please clarify ....
2. How did he/she get on with other staff? ....
3. How did he/she get on with customers? ....
4. What were his/her strong points? ....
5. What were his/her weak points? ....
6. Was he/she honest? .... 7. Was he/she reliable? ....
8. Was he/she industrious? .... 9. Was he/she co-operative? ......
10. Was he/she a good timekeeper? ....
11. How was his/her health? ....
12. What was the reason for leaving? ....
13. Would you re-employ him/her? ....
14. Do you know of any domestic trouble that might affect
    his/her work? ....
15. What is your relationship to the occupant? ....
16. How long have you known him/her? ....
17. Do you believe him/her to be of good character and honest?

Have you any comments regarding the applicant's suitability for the
position of ....

....

Do you know of any reason, not already mentioned, why the
applicant should not be employed by us? ....

....

SIGNED ....

POSITION .... DATE ....

employee has no choice but to accept this figure, although he does have the right to refuse to accept any back payments due to him, if he puts this in writing.

If you are not receiving a copy of the Wages Orders, or have any query relating to it, contact your nearest Wages Inspector at one of the following addresses:

Fiveways House	5th Floor	The Pithay	Companies House
Islington Row	125 Queens Road	Bristol	Crown Way
Middleway	Brighton	BS1 2NQ	Maindy
Birmingham	BN1 3WB	0272 291071	Cardiff
B15 1SP	0273 23333		CF4 3UW
021 643 8191			0222 388588
Pentland House	Franborough Hs	BP House	31 Princes Street
47 Robb's Loan	123-157 Bothwell St	Hemel Hempstead	Ipswich
Edinburgh	Glasgow	Herts	Suffolk
EH14 1UE	G2 7EQ	HP1 1DW	IP1 1ND
031 443 8731	041 248 5427/9	0442 3714	0473 216046
City House	Hanway House	Quay House	Wellbar House
Leeds	Red Lion Square	Quay Street	Gallowgate
LS1 4JH	London	Manchester	Newcastle upon
0532 438232	WC1R 4NH	M3 3JE	Tyne
	01 405 8454	061 832 6506	NE1 4TP
			0632 327575

Lambert House	*The Following Trades Are Covered By Wages Councils*		
Talbot Street	Hairdressers	Newsagents	Furniture
Nottingham	Greengrocers	Hardware	Drapers
NG1 5NR	Tobacconist &	Confectioners	Grocers
0602 417820	Household	Electrics	Bakers

(Chemists, Butchers and Florists are *not* covered)

Wages Councils have been the target of much criticism from small employers, who blamed them for increasing the number of unemployed by imposing minimum wages. Whether you agree or disagree, you cannot dispute the fact that each employee has now become a work unit everywhere, and there is no longer any place for human compassion. The question we should ask ourselves is, 'In a free society, should it be right in all cases, that if an employer offers a wage, and an employee is satisfied with it, it is illegal for that person to work if the agreed wage rate is below that set by the Wages Council?'

I will give an example of what I mean. Many years ago I employed an old age pensioner to keep the shop and rear yard clean and tidy. He was 75 years old, lived alone, and did not need the £5 a week I paid him. He had no set hours, worked very slowly and methodically, but always managed to get the job done in the end. Very often he would come in 'just to tidy up something', and it was sometimes quite a job to persuade him to go home. He worked for the companionship and not the money. Eventually his children arranged for him to go into a home, and he died shortly afterwards. If he were working now, and a Wages Inspector called, he would have had to have been dismissed, because we could not have afforded to pay him for the hours it took him to do the job. What would have happened, as did eventually, was that his job would have disappeared by being broken down into individual tasks which were then allotted to other members of the staff. The only person who would have lost out, would have been the very one the Wages Council purported to protect. As I said earlier, there is no compassion with Wages Inspectors!

The Conservative government issued a consultative paper on the future of Wages Councils in its March 1985 Budget in an attempt to remove unnecessary obstacles to the creation of jobs, and suggested that the time was ripe for Wages Councils to be either completely abolished or made the subject of major reforms. As a result they became more 'streamlined', and are now only responsible for laying down minimum wages for adults of 21 and over. The standard working week is counted as 39 hours — anything above this is generally paid at time and a half. Sunday hours, holidays, and pay for under 21 year olds are now contractual matters, and have nothing to do with Wages Councils.

Employment of Children

The regulations regarding the employment of children are as follows:
(1) Children are not allowed to work until two years below the school-leaving age.
(2) Children are not allowed to work before 7.00 a.m.
(3) Children are not allowed to work after 7.00 p.m.
(4) Children are not allowed to work before the close of school hours on any day they attend school.
(5) Children are not allowed to work for more than two hours on any school day.
(6) Children are not allowed to work for more than two hours on a Sunday.
(7) Children are not allowed to lift, carry, or move anything likely to cause injury.

Self-Employed Staff

If you are thinking of employing staff on a 'self-employed' basis, to avoid NHI contributions, deductions etc., bear in mind that they will eventually be classified according to the law by various criteria, the most important of which are:

(1) Has the employer the right to say not only what has to be done, but how it has to be done?

(2) Does the employer fix the hours for the job, or is it left to the person concerned?

(3) Can the person work for someone else during the week?

Staff Holidays

As previously mentioned, the length and conditions of staff holidays used to be laid down by the Wages Councils. This no longer applies. However, details of the old regulations are shown below as a general guide and easy reference chart for new employees. For instance, if you decide to give just two weeks paid holiday a year, simply halve the figures in the table. Holidays are taken between 1 April of one year, and 31 March of the following year, and are earned according to the length of employment up to April. Twelve months' service qualifies for the full holiday period. The table below should be used for employees who have not been working for a whole year, when the normal holiday period is four weeks. For example, an employee who started work in mid-September (six months), and normally works five days a week, would be entitled to 10 days' holiday.

Number of complete calendar months of employment in year ending 31st March.	Days of holiday if normal week is:				
	six days	five days	four days	three days	two days
12 months	24 days	20 days	16 days	12 days	8 days
11 months	22 days	18 days	15 days	11 days	7 days
10 months	20 days	17 days	13 days	10 days	7 days
9 months	18 days	15 days	12 days	9 days	6 days
8 months	16 days	13 days	11 days	8 days	5 days
7 months	14 days	12 days	9 days	7 days	5 days
6 months	12 days	10 days	8 days	6 days	4 days
5 months	10 days	8 days	7 days	5 days	3 days
4 months	8 days	7 days	5 days	4 days	3 days
3 months	6 days	5 days	4 days	3 days	2 days
2 months	4 days	3 days	3 days	2 days	1 day
1 month	2 days	2 days	1 day	1 day	1 day

Before leaving the subject of staff, I remember being shown a broadsheet intended for the branch managers of an internationally known organisation, and which has stuck in my memory ever since. I have modified it for general shop usage and show it below. It might be an idea to write one out in a similar vein, for the benefit and amusement of your own staff, and keep it permanently displayed.

DO YOU KNOW WHO I AM?

I'm the customer who waits patiently until the staff have finished chatting, before coming to serve me.

I'm the one who would never dream of making any adverse comment about the hygiene in your shop.

I would never dare point out the correct price of an item when I am overcharged or shortchanged.

I would not make any adverse comment about the way the staff never smile at me, and always try to serve someone else first.

Nor would I dare argue when I am abused after mentioning that I did not receive the item I ordered.

THAT'S RIGHT

I'm a jolly good chap, and my wife and our friends are also.

BUT do you know who else I am?

I'M THE CUSTOMER WHO NEVER COMES BACK!

In addition, I cannot understand why you seem to put in so much effort with advertising and special offers and other gimmicks to get me to come into your shop, when I have been there already.

DO YOU REMEMBER ME?

Another notice (if you like notices) might be made out something like the following:

DON'T   moan — customers would rather tell you their troubles than listen to yours.

DON'T   use expressions such as 'What you again?', or 'Where have you been lately?'.

DON'T   anticipate orders from customers.

DON'T   air your views on politics or religion.

DON'T   repeat scandal, or criticise one customer to another.

DON'T   talk to customers too long, when there is work to do.

IT IS BETTER TO BE A GOOD LISTENER THAN A GOOD TALKER.

Administration: Or Keeping Up With The Paperwork

The word 'administration' may conjure up pictures of yourself sitting behind a grandiose desk, smoking a huge cigar, batteries of telephones in front of you, and a copy of *Playboy* in the top drawer. Unfortunately, as far as we are concerned, the word means 'bookwork'. If you are already reaching out to turn the page in order to escape — *STOP*. Bookwork is a necessary evil, and although it may become more evil as time progresses, it is the only means by which you will be able to keep a check on the business and the profits. The only way of keeping the paperwork up straight is to get into a routine, and to set aside certain times of the week for this. The way that suits me best, is to enter cash takings and payments at the close of business daily, and then at the end of the week to make sure that the cash book and any ledgers are brought up to date. If you neglect this, and leave them to accumulate for any length of time, not only will you be unaware of the current trading position, but you probably will also be losing money on expenses that are not entered into the relevant books.

If you have been trained in accountancy, or are that way inclined, I suggest you skip the rest of this section, and buy a book on double entry bookkeeping which will keep you busy to your heart's content. If you are not, and are like the rest of us overworked shopkeepers who are more interested in taking money in the shop than sitting upstairs writing about it, I suggest you follow the ensuing method, making use of a cash book and the filing system described earlier.

Cash Book

I cannot stress too much the importance of getting into a routine and sticking to it, as far as filling in the cash book is concerned. Regardless of the accounting system you use, you must set aside an hour or so each week, preferably at the same time, to keep this book up straight. Once you leave it for a few weeks you are sunk.

Personally, I make sure the cash book is written up and balanced at the close of business each Saturday. I use my own 'CLEAR 'N' EASY TRADERS YEARLY ACCOUNTS BOOK' (illustration overleaf), because I like to spend as little time as possible on this side of the business. But whether you use my system, or Simplex, or Evrite, or Collins etc., you must make sure you fill in all sections — they are all important.

Everyone completes the 'TAKINGS' section, but how many make entries under 'OTHER RECEIPTS', and a year or so later are racking their brains trying to think where 'so and so' came from, in answer to their accountant's questions? Any monies which are not takings should be shown in this column, and a little note written underneath stating their origins. If this is not done, the bank and cash balance sections cannot be filled in properly.

Do not be afraid to alter the headings and purpose of any columns not in use. For example, in my accounts book, as in many others, I have two sections for further rates of VAT. One of these I find ideal to record daily takings of Xmas Club payments which have been rung up on a separate department on the tills. A system like this is essential to save utter confusion with Xmas Club receipts.

Obviously all payments for goods for resale should be entered into the accounts book, and cash payments written down as soon as possible lest they be forgotten, which would result in an inflated gross profit, and a higher income tax demand.

Likewise, careful note should be made of all expenses relevant to the business, because for every £100 worth not listed you will pay at least another £27 income tax.

Always fill in the bank balance section, and update it if necessary, when you receive a bank statement.

The cash balance should also always be completed and the 'cash carried forward' figure checked against the actual cash you have in hand. If there is a discrepancy you have missed something out.

Make sure complete details of any unusual business is included even if it means scribbling in the margin something like 'Lent £250 to Laura, to be repaid by standing order £50 per month'. Remember, the more information you include in your accounts book, the easier it will be for your accountant, and, in theory at least, the cheaper will be his bill.

Another reason to keep your books up straight weekly is to get rid of the quarterly VAT 'headache'. With my accounts book this only takes a few minutes, but whatever system you use, I strongly advise you to complete the return as quickly as possible. After all, if you owe them money you do not have to send it until the end of the month, but if they owe you, why not get it as soon as possible?

Before leaving the accounts book it is worth mentioning that all totals should be entered in pencil until such time as the whole week's balance has been agreed, and then inked in.

The Cardboard Box Filing System

This is described on page 110, and is used instead of a single entry bookkeeping system, which would entail the use of a bought ledger book. I find the cardboard box files give me more information faster, than if I kept a bought ledger. Keep the filing box in the shop, in an easily accessible position, so that deliveries and invoices, breakages and shortages, may be written in with the maximum of ease and the minimum of delay. Do these things immediately. It only takes a couple of seconds, and is just a matter of getting into a routine. Unfortunately, if you leave matters for a few days, thinking you will catch up later, you can just as easily get into a routine of *not* doing it. It is surprising after only a couple of days, how easily items can be forgotten.

Whenever a rep comes to see you for an order or to be paid, the first thing you must do is to bring out his file and check the statement details against yours, and if necessary amend it. This way you will not pay a bill that has been sent to you in error. Computers may be infallible, but those who feed them information are not. You only need a couple of these a year to be well out of pocket. At the end of the week, when you bring your cash book up straight, look at each of the files and pay any amounts that are outstanding and which need to be sent by post.

Occasionally it is necessary to find the financial standing of your business. With the aid of the filing system this is very easy. All you need do is determine the total amount of money owing by you, through looking at each file in turn, and totalling the outstanding balances, and then comparing this to your current bank balance as taken from your cash book. With a good eye for your stock situation, which will come in time, you will soon be able to recognise any warning signs in advance, and take measures to deal with them. If this situation does occur, do not be tempted into buying non-essential items of equipment or extra stock, even though they may look a bargain. There will always be bargains to be found, and you will sleep more easily at night if you only take advantage of these when you have enough money to pay for them.

Another advantage of the filing system is that it is very easy to find

	Period 1 Jan-Mar Budget	Actual	Period 2 Apr-Jun Budget	Actual	6 Month Total Budget	Actual	Period 3 Jul-Sep Budget	Actual	9 Month Total Budget	Actual	Period 4 Oct-Dec Budget	Actual	Total for Year Budget	Actual
Sales	38762	39241	41398	42476	80160	81717	40841		121001		40936		161937	
Less cost of Goods Sold	31387	31746	32167	33132	63554	64878	31285		94839		32135		126984	
Gross Profit	7375	7495	9231	9344	16606	16839	9556		26162		8801		34963	
GP %	19.0	19.1	22.3	22.0	20.7	20.6	23.4		21.6		21.5		21.6	
Rent	500	500	500	500	1000	1000	500		1500		500		2000	
Rates	264	264	265	290	529	554	264		793		265		1058	
Electricity	208	213	271	291	479	504	313		792		225		1017	
Telephone	41	36	42	39	83	75	41		124		42		166	
Insurance	—	—	107	112	107	112	—		107		106		213	
Bank Charges	52	52	53	53	105	105	52		157		53		210	
Repairs etc	66	—	66	347	132	347	66		198		67		265	
Postage	15	12	16	19	31	31	15		46		16		62	
Bags etc	208	221	209	249	417	470	209		626		209		835	
Vehicles exps.	385	410	386	422	771	832	385		1156		386		1542	
Wages	2948	2948	2948	2948	5896	5896	2948		8844		2948		11792	
Cleaning	59	65	60	70	119	135	60		179		60		239	
Sundries	111	110	111	125	222	235	111		333		112		445	
Accountancy	123	123	124	124	247	247	124		371		124		495	
Rental security	102	102	103	103	205	205	102		307		103		410	
HP Interest	119	119	119	119	238	238	119		357		119		476	
Leasing	85	85	86	142	170	227	85		256		85		341	
Depreciation	378	378	378	378	756	756	378		1134		378		1512	
	5664	5638	5844	6631	11508	11969	5772		17280		5798		23078	
Net Profit	1711	1857	3387	3013	5098	4870	3784		8882		3003		11885	

how much you have spent with a supplier over a given period. This is very useful in many ways, one of which is that as time goes by so quickly, you may not actually realise that you have only purchased 'x' amount of goods from a particular supplier in the past six months, say, and may find it beneficial to close that account and obtain the odd required item elsewhere, possibly, because of quantity terms you already qualify for, at a better rate.

One point that should be mentioned at this stage, is that you actually need two cardboard box files. The second need not have any record cards. Simple divisions are enough. Into this box are filed all the relevant invoices and statements that have been agreed and paid. The first box only carries current transactions. In other words, after you have paid a rep or posted a cheque, the paperwork appertaining to that order is not replaced in the first box, but filed later into the second.

The above two items, cash book and cardboard box, are all you need to maintain a satisfactory bookkeeping system, unless you employ staff, in which case you will need to keep a wages book. This is described later under the sub-heading 'Staff Wages Book'. To return to the business side, if you have time, a budgeting analysis book or sheet will prove extremely useful in showing in more detail exactly how the business is progressing. This is not essential, and is not required by your accountant nor by the tax office, but if you wish to have a go, here is one method.

Take a sheet of paper and copy the chart on page 96, which divides the year into four quarters. Next, take a copy of your last financial accounts, or if you have not been there long enough to have completed a full year, a set of accounts from the past owner will do. Divide the sales figure by four, and also all the expense items, and enter them on the analysis sheet in the relevant budget columns as illustrated, but taking into account any seasonal fluctuations. If expenses occur only once or twice a year at the same time, they may be placed in the appropriate quarter's column. The budget figures are your target figures. At the end of each quarter insert the actual amounts, and arrive at a net profit. By comparing this with your budgeted profit, you will be able to ascertain how the business is progressing compared with the previous year. It is not a perfect system, but it takes only a minimal effort four times a year, and provides an early warning system if things are not proceeding as anticipated.

Forecasting Your Sales

After your first year of trading you will be amazed at the accuracy with which you will be able to forecast your turnover for the following week, or any week over the next few months. This is made possible by using a graph similar to the one below. Ensure you leave sufficient room to accommodate future expansion and inflation, and give each year a separate colour so that in future years the trading pattern will become very obvious.

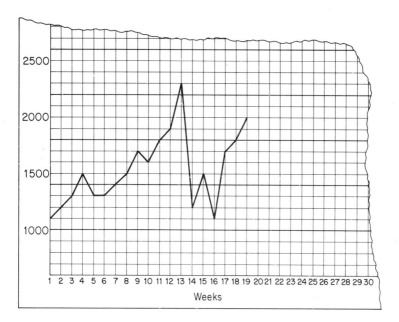

Always be ready to listen to advice. Just as records are made to be broken, so will the system you eventually adopt for your paperwork and general running of the shop be bettered by one more simple, or supplying more information, or both. Be ready to accept it when the opportunity arises. Be flexible in your approach.

Average Transaction Value

This is a useful figure to take note of, and if compared over a period will show any trends in the trade. It is derived by dividing the total sales by the number of transactions. Some modern electronic cash registers provide this figure automatically with the end of the day summary.

Staff Wages Book

If you employ staff you will also have to keep a staff wages book, which will have to be kept up to date and on the premises where it may be inspected by a Wages Inspector, if he happens to call. It need not be anything elaborate, — an ordinary exercise book will do, — but it must contain the name of each employee, the number of hours worked each week, the gross wage for that week, and also any National

Insurance and Income Tax deductions, and the net wage paid. You should also note in this book, for your own benefit, which weeks were taken as holidays, when days were taken off for sickness, and any other time off, including lateness. These records must be kept for three years.

PAYE All employees who are taken on for more than one week must be put onto the PAYE scheme. If they hand you a P45 you are now counted as being their main employer, and you should send Part 3 of the P45 to the Tax Office, and follow the instructions on the Blue Card. If they do not have a P45, either because they have another job or for some other reason, make them complete and sign a P46. If you will be paying them more than the tax-free sum per week, ask them to complete a P15 Coding Claim; send both forms to the Tax Office, and deduct tax on an emergency basis. If pay is below the taxable limit, do not send the P46 to the Tax Office, but keep it in case it may be needed at a later date. If their main employment is elsewhere, send the form to the Tax Office and deduct a straight 30 per cent tax.

National Insurance Contributions If you are self-employed you have to pay two lots of contributions — Class 2, and Class 4.

Class 2 Contributions These are at a flat rate of £3.85 per week at the moment, and are generally increased in April. You do not have to pay this if you are of pensionable age, or your business profits for tax purposes are less than £2,125 for the tax year. Class 2 contributions count for the following benefits:

(1) Basic sickness/invalidity benefit.
(2) Basic widow's benefit.
(3) Basic maternity allowance.
(4) Basic retirement pension.
(5) Child's special allowance.
(6) Death Grant.

They do not count towards unemployment benefit. If you are self-employed you cannot claim unemployment money.

Class 4 contributions These are in reality an extra tax from which the self-employed derive no benefit at all. It is assessed at the same time the Inland Revenue computes your tax liability, and is based on the amount of profit you have earned. The rates generally alter in April, and are at the moment 6.3 per cent of taxable profits between £4,590 and £15,340 per year. If there is a partnership of husband and wife, the Class 4 contribution will be assessed on each partner's share of the profits. Tax relief will be allowed on half of this contribution.

Pensions If you are self-employed all you can look forward to when you retire is the basic state pension unless you contribute to a private pension plan. There are many different types of these, run by insurance companies in the main, but basically are either paid by regular monthly instalments, or lump sums once a year when your annual profits are known. They all have the added benefit of being allowed against your top rate of tax, and provide either a sizeable lump sum plus a weekly pension for the rest of your life, or a weekly pension only, at a higher rate, once you reach retirement age. The only drawback is that you cannot make use of the money until then.

You and the Boss

Before we leave the topic of staff, just a word about your own position as an employer. When I was much younger I used to run a restaurant and snack bar in my parents' pub. One of my regular customers came in about three times a week and always asked for two rounds of roast beef sandwiches to take away, for his guv'nor. He always stressed that his guv'nor only liked lean meat, and that so long as the quality of the sandwiches remained high, he would continue to be sent in for them.

One day he asked for the sandwiches as usual, and then proceeded to eat them at the bar with a drink. I asked him what he thought he was doing, eating his guv'nor's sandwiches. He replied, patting his stomach, 'My guv'nor is extra hungry today, and can't wait any longer!'

You may now ask 'What has all this to do with running a business?' The answer is very simple. It was much easier for my customer to say that his guv'nor did not want fat in his sandwiches, and that if there was any fat he would not buy any more, than for him to say it was for himself. This way there was no confrontation. He was passing the buck, but getting the results. He had the best of both worlds.

You can make this work for you, just as I have done on occasions in the past, in order to get out of an awkward or compromising situation. Take the case of a salesman who offers, on the face of it, what appears to be a very good deal, but about which you have a few nagging doubts. If you play safe and say 'no' there and then, you may miss out on a very good genuine opportunity. If you say 'yes' immediately, you stand a very good chance of losing your money. If however, you tell the salesman that you like the idea, are not authorised to make such a decision, and on no account can you make any payments without such authorisation, but you will note down all the relevant details, and will contact him after you have spoken to your guv'nor, you have a get-out. It will stop the salesman trying to close the deal with you, and will give you the opportunity of checking on the firm. The salesman will know this will happen, and if there is anything underhand, the odds are that you will never see him again anyway.

You can take the 'guv'nor' image as far as you like. In fact there is no need for any of the staff or customers to know that there is not a

r' who has the last word. This can save some embarras-
with those customers who may ask you to change a
haps lend them ten pounds until the end of the week. If
…ౖe told that you have strict instructions not to do this, and that
your guv'nor checks the banking with the tills, you are able to refuse
with no hard feelings.

If the staff are under this illusion also, you may find it easier to
change their hours, or introduce unpopular regulations when necessary. It depends on your personal make-up. If you like to call a spade a
spade, and enjoy confrontations, then fine. If you want to get things
done in the easiest manner, with the least bother, you may find that the
'Guv'nor' will work for you. After all, it is how orders are passed on in
big business!

Pricing and Profit Margins

Anyone can increase their takings by selling goods at low prices. In
fact, if you sold all your goods at cost, you would have a fantastic
turnover for the size of your shop, and earn no profit. On the other
hand, the public expect to see a certain number of special offers, even if
they do not buy them, and the shop that has no offers, although it
works on a good gross profit percentage, is not working to its full
potential. The exception to this is the specialist shop where people are
more concerned with the quality than the price.

What we have to do then, is to find the happy medium. To do this
we have to understand the effect special offers have on profit margins,
and more importantly, on *cash profit*.

For this purely hypothetical exercise we shall assume that all
expenses remain the same apart from staff wages. This is not strictly
accurate, because the busier you are, the more paper bags and till rolls
etc., you will use, and the more wear and tear there is on equipment
such as scales, machinery and cash registers. However, as these factors
vary between different trades, we shall ignore them and only consider
the staff wage bill as varying with turnover. We shall take a figure of 6
per cent of turnover as the appropriate ratio, although this varies
obviously with different trades. It will be easy enough to substitute
your own profit margins and staff wages in the examples below. The
actual figures do not matter. It is the principle that counts.

		The Effects on Net Profits when too many Special Offers are sold				
Takings including S/Offers @ 18% GP @ 3% GP		Overall Gross Profit	Expenses	Staff	Gross Profit	Net Profit
1000	—	18%	50	60	180	70
1000	200	15%	50	60	150	40
1000	300	13½%	50	60	135	25
1000	400	12%	50	60	120	10
1000	450	11¼%	50	60	112	2

From this you will see the disastrous effect selling too many special offers can have. The next table shows what sort of increase in trade you need, to result in the same net profit.

Takings including S/Offers @ 18% GP @ 3% GP		Overall Gross Profit	Expenses	Staff	Gross Profit	Net Profit
1000	—	18%	50	60	180	70
1130	100	16.6%	50	68	188	70
1250	200	15.6%	50	75	195	70
1370	300	14.7%	50	82	201	70
1500	400	14%	50	90	210	70

and so on. In other words, for every £100 worth of special offers you sell, you need to take an *extra* £130 to end up with the same net profit. Anything above this will be extra profit at 18 per cent. There is an added benefit also, in that as most businesses for sale tend to be priced on turnover rather than profit, the shop value will be higher. Many vendors take advantage of this fact when about to place their shops on the market, and push lots of special offers to increase the takings.

Special offers or 'price cutting' is particularly prevalent in the grocery trade, and unless some control is exercised in the selection of the number of these and the type, you could very easily find yourself working at a loss. Fortunately nowadays, with the advent of computers, wholesalers are able to provide invoices which not only suggest retail prices of all their goods, but also work out the overall gross profit percentage of the goods if sold at those prices. If these prices are adhered to, and everthing else is sold at the normal price, it is very simple to work out fairly accurately what your gross profit percentage should be, and thus your actual gross profit cash per week. This method applies to all types of trades, not just grocers. The grocery trade is specifically mentioned because on the face of it, with profit margins ranging from one per cent or less to over 35 per cent in a few cases, it would seem at first glance to be practically impossible to work out.

Before we can start talking about gross profit margins however, we have to know what 'gross profit' means, and how to work it out. There are two types of gross profit. There is 'gross profit on return', and 'gross profit on cost'.

Gross Profit on Cost

This is the profit margin non-shopkeepers and some reps talk about. It is the profit earned on the price charged to you by the manufacturers or wholesaler and is calculated as follows: *profit/cost* × 100.

For example, if you buy an item for £5 and sell it for £10 (5/5 x 100) = 100, you are said to earn 100 per cent profit. That is 100 per cent of the cost price. If you sell the same article for £8 (3/5 × 100) = 60, you earn 60 per cent. On the other hand if you sell it for £25 (20/5 × 100) = 400, you will earn 400 per cent profit. Obviously you can have very large fluctuations in profit margins by this method, and the drawback is that it involves more complicated arithmetic to find out how much you have earned from your takings, because this method is based on the cost price and not the selling one. The reason reps talk about this system often, is because profit margins based on the cost price are always larger than those based on the selling price. The cash profit is the same of course, but it sounds better from their point of view.

Gross Profit on Return

This is the profit margin based on the price the goods are sold at, and is worked out by the following formula: *profit/selling price* × 100. Therefore an item bought for £5 and sold for £10 (5/10 × 100) = 50 per cent, and if it were sold for £8 it would be (3/8 × 100) = 37 ½ per cent, and if it were sold for £25 it would be ($^{20}/_{25}$ × 100) = 80 per cent.

By this method it is impossible to earn 100 per cent, unless the goods cost you nothing, because 100 per cent represents the selling price. This method is used by shopkeepers, because once you know what sort of percentage profit you are working on, you can very easily translate your daily takings into cash profit. For instance, if you are working on 18 per cent GP (Gross Profit), and you take £490 in the shop, you know you should have earnt £88 (490/18 × 100). Sums like these are child's play now that almost everyone owns a pocket calculator.

Here are a few short cuts that may prove useful if remembered:

Double cost price = 50% on return
Add ½ to cost price = 33.3% on return
Add ⅓ to cost price = 25% on return
Add ¼ to cost price = 20% on return
Add ⅕ to cost price = 16.6% on return
Add ⅙ to cost price = 14.3% on return
Add ⅒ to cost price = 9% on return

Having discovered what is meant by gross profit, we shall now return to the original problem of finding out the average gross profit of a typical shop. The first thing you have to do is list all your suppliers and check back over a period of say, ten weeks (simply because it is easier to divide by ten), to find the average amount spent with each per week. It may be necessary with some suppliers who deliver very infrequently, to go back over a much longer period. Next, check the invoices to find the average gross profit percentage from each supplier. In all probability you will not have to check many invoices from the same supplier, because the profit margins will be very similar. Just to recap on how to determine the gross profit percentage from a supplier's invoice:

(1) Extend each item at retail prices, to find the total retail value of the invoice, taking into account any wastage involved.
(2) Subtract the invoice value from the retail value, to arrive at the gross profit.
(3) Divide the retail value into the gross profit and multiply by 100, to give the percentage.

Example

(1) Retail value of invoice £29.48
(2) Subtract invoice value £23.64 = £5.84 profit
(3) Divide this figure by the retail value and multiply by
100 — (5.84/29.48 × 100) = 19.8 per cent.

Beside each supplier write the average amount spent, and the gross profit percentage. Then extend this to arrive at a retail figure by deducting the gross percentage from 100, dividing the average invoice value by this figure, and then multiplying by 100. It sounds far more complicated than it is. The above example would work like this:

$$100 — 19.81 = 80.19$$
$$23.64/80.19 × 100 = £29.48$$

After following this formula for each of your suppliers, you should end up with a chart such as the one below.

All Figures Weekly			
Supplier	Average Invoice	Percentage Profit	Retail Value
Bloggs Sausages	37.45	18%	45.67
Smith's Shirtbuttons	9.30	50%	18.60
Spuds Greengrocery	128.60	23%	167.01
Main Wholesaler	1,473.00	13%	1,693.10
Ferdie's Fridges	341.00	25%	454.66
Greetings Cards	18.20	45%	33.09
Merlin's Medicines	60.90	35%	93.69
TOTAL	2,068.45		2,505.83

Using our formula:

(2505,83 — 2068.45)/2505.83 × 100 = 17.45% Gross Profit

By applying this percentage to our weekly takings, we can now determine what our cash profit per week should be. For instance, if one week your takings amount to £2,867.93, then you should have earned £500.45 (2867.93 × 17.45%). If you compare this figure with that shown on your yearly accounts you will have some idea of how much is being pilfered by customers/staff. A watchful eye can also be kept on profits during the year by having regular stock checks, and comparing. This has the dual benefit of nipping any shortages in the bud, and also making it clear to the staff that you are keeping a close eye on the profits.

If your *Gross Profit* percentage is lower than it should be, it could be from one of the following causes:

(a) Dipping into the till by yourself, your family, or your staff. Check on each in turn, not only for cash disappearing, but also for goods. It is very easy to take items from the shop and not pay for them, but you must realise that this will reduce your gross profit in exactly the same way as if they had been stolen.
(b) Stock being wasted, damaged or stolen.
(c) Bad buying of stock that does not sell, and has to be cleared at cost price, or even below.
(d) Not taking sufficient notice of current price lists, and marking goods up at old prices, whilst paying more for them yourselves.
(e) Shoplifting (covered elsewhere).
(f) Delivery men.

If your *Net Profit* percentage is lower than it should be, checking is easier, because it will have to be the result of increases in overheads such as staff, telephone, rent, rates, vehicle expenses, electricity etc. Some of these items you will have no control over, e.g. rent and rates, but others should be looked at closely to see if any savings can be made.

Achieving Your Estimated Gross Profit

If you buy goods which you intend to sell for £100, and which cost you £75, you expect to make £25 or 25 per cent profit. You must understand that this is your *maximum* profit. It is *not* the percentage you will finish with. This will be influenced by factors such as pilferage, breakages, wastage, deterioration, and obsolesence. Your efficiency will be judged by how near your final gross profit figure is to your estimated one. Remember also, that this figure can only go down, and vigilance must be exercised from the moment the goods are delivered to you, to the time when you actually pay for them with the money the customers have spent in your shop, and you have then banked. Your first job then, is to ensure the delivery man leaves your correct order.

Checking in Goods The following procedure should be employed every time you have a delivery.

(1) Check that the delivery is actually for you, from the address at the top of the delivery note or invoice.
(2) Take note of the condition of the outers (boxes), and if any are damaged either refuse them or write a few words to that effect on the delivery note.
(3) Check that the total number of outers is correct, and sign it 'unexamined'.
(4) Make sure the delivery man leaves the shop *empty-handed*.
(5) Check goods against delivery note or invoice, and make a note of any shortages or damages on your file, and telephone the company concerned if necessary.

'Your First Loss is Your Best Loss'

This maxim was told to me many years ago, and it still holds good. Two typical examples of this are as follows:

(1) An item of fresh food is not selling, and is nearing the end of its life. It has cost you £1, and is on sale at £1.40. If you reduce the price to 99p you will probably sell it straight away, and virtually get your money back. Reducing by just 10p or so will probably have no effect, and in a few days time you have to throw the item away, and lose £1.
(2) You are selling a 'fad' item that has been the latest craze, and now looks as if it is coming to an end either by market saturation or the advent of a new fad, and you are still holding a lot of stock. In these circumstances it is better to accept the profit you have already made and clear the rest of your stock at near cost price to save you carrying a lot of dead stock for years, and also enabling you to buy the latest 'fad' with your original stock money.

When setting selling prices of goods which are liable to deterioration or evaporation, such as fresh fruit, mushrooms, ham etc., take this into account. For instance, say you want 25 per cent gross profit from an 11 lb tinned ham, you might work it out in the following manner:

Gross Weight 11 lb.
Cost Price 80 lb. = *£8.80* = *£1.06 per lb. to show 25%*

Juice/fat/skin 6 oz.
Waste on m/c 6 oz.
Evaporation 3 oz.   15 oz.

Therefore selling weight = 10lb 1oz @ £8.80 = 87.5p 'real' cost per lb.
= £1.16 per lb. to show 25%. £1.06 per lb would actually show 17½
per cent.

Ordering Larger Quantities

One method of cutting the price of a popular line, and still maintaining
your profit margin, is by ordering larger quantities at cheaper prices,
and deducting the overall additional discount from just one or two
lines. For example, if you normally sell twenty outers a fortnight from
a particular manufacturer at the recommended RSP of 50p per item,
your order may look something like:

Line A — 4 outers. Other — 16 assorted.
Outers contain one dozen units. All outers are the same price. RSP 50p
The quantity rates are as follows:
20 outer rate — (18 per cent) cost 41p × 12 = £4.92 per outer. 60 outer
rate — (30 per cent) cost 35p × 12 = £4.20 per outer.
If five weeks supply is ordered instead, you could order the following:

Line A — 20 outers. Others — 40 assorted.
Total cost 60 × 4.20 = £252.00
Required profit 20 per cent. Therefore total selling price   = £315.00
40 assorted sold at normal retail 40 × 12 × 50p   = £240.00
Therefore 20 outers of Line A needs to sell for   75.00
or 75 / 20 / 12 = 31 ¼p each, or 2 for 63p!
   In fact you will be selling these at less than the 60 outers wholesale
rate!
   This is a hypothetical case of course, but the principle remains the
same where goods are ordered on quantity rates. It is best if this
method can be used on lines that do not conflict with others similar in
the shop, because a good proportion of the increased sales will come at
the expense of your other lines.

Rate of Stock Turn (RST)

One often hears the term 'Rate of Stock Turn' mentioned. This is the
number of times a year you turn over your average amount of stock
carried in the shop. Obviously if you carry sufficient stock for six
months sales, your Stock Turn is two — you will be turning over your
stock twice a year. To find out your own stock turn, work out the
following equation with a calculator:

$$\frac{48 \times \text{weekly takings}}{\text{Average stock}} = \text{RST}$$

(Both figures must be at either cost price, or selling price)

For example, if your takings are £2,600 per week, and your average retail stock values is £9,000, your equation is

$$\frac{48 \times 2,600}{9,000} = \text{Stock turn of } 13.8$$

or, if your takings are £3,000 per week, and your stock is £43,000, you get:

$$\frac{48 \times 3,000}{43,000} = \text{stock turn of } 3.35$$

From this you will see that the higher the RST, the easier it is to sell the goods, and generally, the lower the percentage of profit obtained. Conversely, if you have to carry a large selection of high-value items, you need a larger percentage of profit on your invested capital to offset the low RST. The more often the stock is turned over, the less capital is needed to be tied up.

I remember, many years ago, when I owned a confectioner's and tobacconist, I had a direct account with a confectionery manufacturer. Orders were placed every two months with the rep who was one of these high-powered tape-recording type salesman, and who one day said that our rate of stock turn was six per year, but if we could increase that to seven per year, we would sell more and earn more profit. I asked him how I could increase my stock turn (there was a minimum order), and he replied, 'By increasing your sales'. Again, I asked him how to increase my sales, and he suggested removing another three feet of the opposition's counter display bars, and replacing them with his own products. I did not take him up on his suggestion, because I thought any increase in his sales would be at the expense of other lines, and any increase in his profit margin would be to the detriment of the other profit margins. I leave you to ponder the pros and cons of the argument, and give yet another example for you to think about.

Let us assume we spend £80 per week with each of four suppliers, and another £60 with an assortment of others. Out total spending per week is 4 × 80 + 60 = £380. With quantity rates as below we would earn £75 (455-380).

£50	£80	£120	£200	£250
14%	17%	19%	23%	26%

If the buying pattern were altered to £280 spent with one supplier, and the other £100 spent at the various minimum rates, we would earn £110 (494-380). I leave you to pick holes in the argument. But you must agree it is worth thinking about.

Buying

To make sales you have to have stock. What is generally not realised by the public is that the majority of sales come from a very few lines. The rest are there more or less to give the customer the illusion that he has a very large choice. This applies to all types of trades.

As an example, take a newsagent's. He may carry at least 200 varieties and sizes of chocolate, but the majority of sales will probably come from about 20 lines. The same applies to cigarettes. Actually, in 1971 *half* the total amount of cigarettes sold were accounted for by just two brands — Embassy and No. 6. Newspapers will be the same, depending on whether you are in a *Telegraph* and *Express* area, or a *Mirror* and *Sun*. Ice cream and lollies are another example, as are ladies' tights.

In a grocery shop, from a selection of perhaps 50 different cheeses, at least 20 per cent of sales will probably come from Cheddar. In a post office, first- and second-class stamps may account for over 90 per cent of stamp sales, and £10 postal orders probably sell as many as all the other denominations added together. In a jeweller's window you may have a choice of twelve watches. In all probability not more than three of these will sell to any degree, the others not being duplicated inside, and probably 90 per cent of sales coming from the three popular models. This presents the problem of stock control in its proper perspective. In reality, the jeweller need only have three designs of watch, but his sales would greatly dimish if the customer did not think that he had a large choice. In other words, proper stock control depends on giving the impression of carrying a very wide range, but having by far the majority of your money tied up in the fast-selling lines, which you must make sure you never run out of. If 10 per cent of your lines produce over 50 per cent of your sales, this means that 90 per cent of your lines account for less than half your sales. You should therefore continually strive to reduce that 90 per cent figure, because this will show natural growth as new lines are introduced, the majority of which will not achieve sustained sales.

Being Out of Stock: this results in lost sales immediately, and also possibly in the future, if customers are dissatisfied. Careful checking at regular intervals will reduce 'out of stocks' to a minimum, but there are some occasions when it is inevitable. One such occasion is when a recipe, or an article recommending a particular item, appears in a local or national paper unexpectedly, and everyone rushes out to buy. Care should be taken when re-ordering these goods. Another occasion is if you have a school nearby, and the cookery lesson calls for 4 oz of a particular food that sells very slowly. Suddenly you may have 30 people asking for it, because none of the mothers have any at home. There is a solution to this however, and also a possible boost to turnover, if the home economics teacher is approached and some type of formula mutually arrived at.

Yet another source of being out of stock is the panic-buying syndrome, initiated by a newspaper article which states that such and such a product might soon be unavailable. In recent years this has resulted in housewives stocking up with sufficient salt and pepper to last the rest of their lives, and ending up with pounds of damp sugar. In this latter case, of course, if supplies are limited and are likely to remain so for some time, quantities as large as possible should be ordered from many sources, because people will buy it if they see it, even if they do not need it, just in case someone else ends up with more.

Being In Stock: try to find the happy medium. If you over-order on too many lines you may encounter wastage, and will certainly end up with cash flow problems, which may force you to sell up even though you have good sales.

As we have previously stated, gross profit is the difference between the price you buy at, and the price you sell at. Too many people tend to forget this, and concentrate solely on the selling price, automatically reducing this whenever they are able to buy cheaper. In many cases this is not necessary, and will not increase sales, but only decrease profits.

Begin by buying the same goods from the same suppliers, to ensure the same price and quality, until you are conversant enough with the trade to start experimenting yourself. If you are told by a supplier that there has been an increase in the price of an article, and a similar article is available elsewhere, do not be afraid to buy from an alternative source. Remember, no manufacturer or wholesaler is doing you a favour by supplying you. You are free to buy from whatever source you wish, and may get a better price if you make this known to the supplier. Do not be afraid to bargain on larger quantities. They can only say 'No'.

You must have some sort of filing system for delivery notes, invoices, statements, price lists, and records of orders for each supplier. There is no need to buy anything elaborate to house these in if you do not wish to. I made do with an old cardboard box, with a cardboard division and record card for each supplier, similar to the illustration below, for years.

The record card is two-sided. One side is used for delivery and payment details, and the other for ordering. The remarks section should be used to write down short deliveries, breakages etc., and is a most useful memory aid for when reps come round.

The other side of the card should be ruled off as below, and used for taking stock and ordering individual lines. S = stock at above date. O

	4/2		3/3		5/4		4/5													
	S	O	S	O	S	O	S	O	S	O	S	O	S	O	S	O	S	O	S	O
Pork 8's	6	15	4	15	2	16	3	15												
Pork Chops ½lb	2	9	2	9	–	12	2	10												
Pork & Beef 8's	4	7	3	7	1	9	4	4												
Pork & Beef Chps ½lb	3	6	5	1	1	5	2	4												
Beef 8's	1	10	3	7	–	12	1	12												
Pork 6/lb	2	14	2	14	3	12	1	15												
Pork & Beef 6/lb	1	18	4	13	2	14	–	18												

= order. The system is very simple to use. The first order is an educated guess. The second order is determined by adding your previous stock to your last order, and deducting your present stock. This will tell you the amount of outers you have sold since your last order. Deduct your present stock from the number of outers you have sold, add an additional amount, which will depend on the length of time it takes to receive the order, and that will be your new order. If the delivery comes off the van, there is no need to add an allowance. Again, it sounds far more complicated writing about it, than it is in practice.

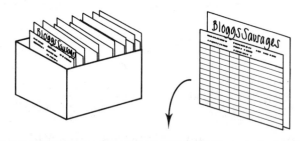

Supplier	Bloggs Sausages			Rep. A. Chipolata		Tel. 000 000
Address	Banger St			¼ Weekly Call		
	Sausage City					
Order Date	Delivery Date	Invoice Amount	Date Paid	Amount Paid	Remarks	
4/2	9/2	37·42	3/3	37·42		
3/3	8/3	42·61	5/4	40·51	1 x Pack Short 2 x Damaged	
5/4	10/4	48·73	4/5	48·73		
4/5	11/5	63·20			No Free Gift !	

As an example, we will take 'Pork 8's' above. On 4 February there were six outers in stock, and fifteen ordered. A month later, on 3 March, there were four outers left. This meant that 17 outers had been sold in that time. As we have four outers left, we only need 13 outers, but we will order 15 to avoid being out of stock before the next delivery arrives.

Always check the invoice against the delivery note, and the statement against the invoice, before paying any accounts.

Do not look on reps as being a nuisance. If they call at an awkward or busy time, arrange for a more convenient time in future. If you feel unsure about trying a new line, ask the rep to supply you with a small trial sample. Make use of reps. They spend all day travelling round shops, both large and small, looking at different layouts and displays, and can make some useful suggestions. If you want advice, and they are unable to provide the answer, they will generally go out of their way to find it. After all, their livelihood and commission depends on you.

Order seasonal goods early and do not place too large an order. Items such as Christmas crackers left after Christmas, and Easter eggs after Easter, are a dead loss, and either hang around until next year, or have to be reduced in price. If you sell out of a certain line beforehand, you can always buy something similar to replace it with. The advantage of ordering early is that you are offered a full range of goods to choose from. If you leave it until later in the year, other retailers will have taken all the best lines, and you will be left to choose from the goods nobody else wants. Some wholesalers and manufacturers will deliver Christmas lines a few months beforehand, and not require payment until Christmas. They think that their goods will stand a better chance of being sold whilst in your shop, than in their warehouse. It will be of benefit to you if you seek out suppliers who are willing to offer this service. On the other hand, ordering early does not mean that you have to accept delivery early. For instance, you could order Easter eggs in November, and ask for delivery in February, in good time for Easter.

In many trades if you order goods monthly, the invoices are payable by the end of the month following delivery. To give yourself the longest credit, order most goods at the beginning of the month.

Quantity Discounts

Many firms offer extra discounts for larger orders. These may be in the form of an extra percentage discount if you order over a certain amount, such as an extra 10 per cent if the value of your order exceeds £200, or they may be by the step method. This is where each item has a different price for different quantities, the total amount ordered determining the group pricing. The method is illustrated below.

If one outer (box) of each were ordered, you would be charged Group A prices for each item.

Retail price each	Group						
	A 1-5	B 6-10	C 11-20	D 21-35	E 36-60	F 61-100	G 100+
Chocolate eclairs (12) 28p	2.86	2.76	2.69	2.52	2.35	2.18	2.02
Bath buns (12) 20p	2.04	1.97	1.92	1.80	1.68	1.56	1.44
Cream doughnuts (12) 16p	1.63	1.57	1.54	1.44	1.34	1.25	1.16
Eccles (12) 22p	2.24	2.16	2.11	1.98	1.84	1.72	1.59
Dundee (singles) £3	2.55	2.46	2.40	2.25	2.10	1.95	1.80

If you placed the following order:
·1 × eclairs, 6 × Bath buns, 10 doughnuts, 4 × Dundee cakes, you would pay group D prices for *each*, because the total number of outers ordered is 21. When ordering, I have found it best to pencil in the required order, total it, and then decide whether it is best to add a couple of outers or so, to go for the next group. If you do this, it is *always* best to make up the extra outers from the best selling line/s, rather than look through the price list for an additional line which you will probably have to make room for and utlimately be stuck with.

Do not be lured into buying far more than you can reasonably sell if there is any possibility of the goods deteriorating, or being out of date, or out of fashion before you can sell them.

Stockroom Control

Possibly one of the most time-consuming exercises in a shop is the replenishing of goods on to display shelving from the stockroom area. This usually consists of an unending number of trips backwards and forwards, and inevitably a number of lines that cease to be offered in the shop and are displayed solely in the stock room.

The goods in the stockroom are initially put there of course when an outer of, say, 24 items is delivered and there is only room for 12 on the shop shelf. The remaining 12 are put into the stockroom and kept for topping up as necessary.

There is a very simple method for controlling this, and ensuring the shop shelves are as full as possible. First, take an exercise book and divide the pages as in the following illustration, or draw out the format and have several sheets photocopied.

Next, in column (1) write a description of the goods taken into the stockroom. Column (2) contains the number of items. 'P' stands for 'plenty', i.e. too many to count quickly. The following columns are used to enter the number of items needed in the shop. When all of a particular line has been taken out, it is ruled through.

To use: walk round the shop with the sheet or sheets, writing into the next available column the number of items that will fit into the shop display shelf.

If you have a very varied stock you will be amazed at how much time this system saves, and how much fuller your shelves will appear.

(1)	(2)																					
Proc. Peas A1	11	4	3																			
" " A2	16	2	1																			
Baked Beans Sm	21	1																				
~~" " Med~~	~~9~~	~~6~~	~~5~~																			
" " Lge	6																					
~~Orange Sq 1 litre~~	~~4~~	~~2~~	~~2~~																			
" " 2 litre	3																					
Lemon Sq 1 litre	2	1																				
Men's Tissues	7	1																				
Coloured "	2	1																				
Exercise Books	18	3	4																			

Voluntary Buying Groups and Symbol Groups

Voluntary groups, in their present form, were created in the 1950s to help the independent retailer combat the increasing threat from the explosion of supermarkets and multiple chains. The groups were formed by a wholesaler with a number of retailers, and then chains were formed by several wholesalers combining to serve many retailers under the same banner.

Nowadays they are very sophisticated in their approach, and provide special offers, window posters, general advice, and guidance on store layout and development. These items are paid for by the individual retailer who is levied a weekly charge, which varies between groups, and generally, although not always, is linked to the service you get.

Apart from the well known voluntary groups in the grocery trade such as Spar, Londis, Maceline, VG, etc., there are several other voluntary groups serving chemists, confectioners, tobacconists, hardware shops, and others.

Cash and Carry Warehouses

These also originated in the 1950s, and are able to offer better prices because they make savings on clerical staff, reps, transport, credit facilities, and bad debts. They also offer the advantage of being able to buy smaller outers.

Both independent stores and members of buying groups are using the cash and carry more and more because of the very competitive prices offered. The big advantage, apart from price, is the range of stock carried. This means that if they are out of stock of the particular brand you are looking for, you will usually be able to find a substitute, and not lose sales from being out of stock. The big disadvantage is, as the name implies, the fact that you have to pay cash then and there for any goods you buy. The big bone of contention, with many a cash and carry, is the apparent ease with which the public are able to obtain a card to allow them in. It is very annoying and frustrating for a shopkeeper to be standing shoulder to shoulder with one of his customers at the cash point, having bought the same item, when he knows full well that his customer has no connection with the trade at all.

Difficulty in Paying Bills

If you run into a bad patch and get behind with your payments to one or two companies, the best thing for you to do is to telephone or write to the company concerned explaining the position, and offering to repay the outstanding amount by instalments over a set period. Most firms will accept this, because they know that if they took you to court, and it came out that you had made an offer to pay, the court would not take very kindly to their action, and in all probability would make them pay all the costs, and possibly order you to repay even less than you had originally offered. Besides this, the firm concerned will be more interested in helping you get back on your feet so that you can continue to trade with them, and buy their goods.

Disputes Over Charges

It is good practice in cases where there are disagreements over the charges for work done, to pay half the bill, and then argue over the remainder. This may be taken as a goodwill gesture to show that you are not disputing the whole of the bill.

Stocktaking

Stocktaking has to be done yearly at the end of your tax year for audit purposes in order to provide a value for the stock, and thus a gross profit figure for the year. It allows you to see how much money has disappeared during the year by comparing the 'book value' to that of the actual stock. It is a good opportunity to appraise the proportions or selection of stock, and to clear out any extremely slow-moving or obsolete lines. It also provides an accurate figure for the opening stock for the following year, and a guide for insurance purposes. Stocktaking may be done by a professional stocktaker, who will usually charge somewhere between 1 per cent and 4 per cent of the final value of the stock, or you can do it yourself. If you choose the latter, the following method is recommended.

(1) Two days before the stocktaking date, remove sufficient stock from your stockroom, on to the shelves and counters in the actual shop area.

(2) Do not arrange for any stock to be delivered during this two-day period. If a delivery which you particularly need does arrive, place it separately in the stockroom. You then have the choice of including it in your current year's trading together with the relevant invoices, or leaving it until the next.

(3) During the two-day period, count all the stock in the stockroom.

(4) During the selected day for stocktaking, areas of the shop which are particularly slow-moving should have their stock counted whilst the shop is open.

(5) After close of business, the rest of the shop stock on the fixtures should be counted systematically, left to right, top to bottom, on sheets which are headed with the relevant shop position, so that there is no query later as to whether a particular part of the shop has been checked or not. These need only take the form of L/H wall, R/H wall, Back wall, L. gondola, Front display counter, Dairy cabinet, etc.

(6) Stock may be listed at cost price, at selling price, or a combination of both.

(7) Where possible list at cost price.

(8) Have a final check round the shop for odd corners, shop windows, etc. to make sure everything has been counted.

(9) Translate the value of the stock into one of cost price by reducing selling prices by an estimated gross profit percentage, and adding to your cost pricings.

(10) When counting stock you may find it beneficial to use the following method.

Counting in fives — JHH   Counting in sixes — X̲

Book Debts

The easy answer on how to handle book debts, is not to have them in the first place. Newspaper deliveries are an exception, because you cannot reasonably expect people to pay for their papers in advance, but even with these, a careful eye must be kept on them and regular checks made to ensure all accounts are paid up to date.

As far as other forms of credit are concerned, nobody would expect to be able to walk into Tesco's, Sainsbury's, W. H. Smith, Woolworth's or Boots, and be given goods against their promise of paying the following day, even though all these stores could well afford the odd loss far greater than you. On top of all this, in the majority of cases, the people who ask for credit are the ones who do their main shopping elsewhere, spend all their cash in the other store, and then ask you to give them credit so that they may finish their shopping.

Over the years I have always tried to keep this type of transaction to an absolute minimum apart from very odd occasions such as if a regular customer who I knew well, wished to do their shopping on a Thursday, but did not get paid until Friday evening. I have, however, been 'caught' twice in the past 20 years. This may not seem much, but it is twice more than is necessary. I will relate the circumstances leading to these, in the hope that it will make you think *three* times in future when asked, instead of twice.

The first occasion was in 1971 when I was asked by the husband of one of my full-time employees, who had worked for me for several years, if I would lend him £10 for a couple of days. I made all the usual excuses, such as having just been to the bank, and needing what cash I had to pay for deliveries later in the day, etc., but he kept on imploring me, saying his wife knew nothing of the fact that he was in a bit of a fix, and even going so far as to offer me his large garnet signet ring as security.

Eventually I relented, (my first mistake), declined his ring (my second mistake), and promised not to tell his wife (my third mistake). Needless to say, I never saw him nor the money again. The lesson to be learned from this is that, if I had accepted his ring I would have had my money returned. Therefore, if customers want to treat you like a bank, act like a bank. Ask for some security that has a greater value than the amount you are lending.

The second time was when I was approached by a stranger in my grocer's shop, who told me he was a teacher, was on a monthly salary, and wished to open a monthly account to be paid for immediately he received his cheque. I told him that I did not give monthly accounts on principle, apart from the cash flow problems it created. As I was speaking to him, one of my young assistants, who had been working for me for about three years since leaving school, happened to walk by, and was greeted by the stranger. It transpired that he had been one of her teachers whilst she was at school, and after a conversation with her about him, I agreed to his request. After all, if you cannot trust a teacher, who can you trust?

All went well for five months, and then he disappeared owing me just over £50. There was no reply when I called round his house, and I eventually took out a county court summons against him, to which he pleaded guilty and offered to pay £2 per week. I never received a penny of this, because he subsequently disappeared completely from the area, and I learned that the house he was living in had been rented.

I hope the above two examples will serve as sufficient warning of the perils of giving credit, in even the most secure of situations.

Customer Relations

It is as well to be prepared with a ready made answer for the awkward customer, such as the one who comes into your shop shouting out 'I've got a complaint!'. I usually take one step backward, put a shocked expression on my face, and reply 'I hope it's not catching!' This normally takes the seriousness out of the situation, and allows it to be settled amicably.

The following have also been tried and tested, and are recommended.

CUSTOMER 'Why is this packet of Brand X 25p this week, when it was only 19p last week? I think it's disgusting putting your price up 6p in one week. Especially for the old age pensioners, how can they afford it? You should be reported.'

SHOPKEEPER 'Madam, our price for Brand X is 25p. Last week we had a special offer and reduced the price by 6p. This week we have reduced the price of something else.'

SHOPKEEPER (At the checkout) 'That is 30p please.'

CUSTOMER 'No it isn't. It is only 28p. That is what I was charged yesterday.'

SHOPKEEPER 'The correct price is 30p. If you were charged 28p yesterday, you owe me 2p.'

CUSTOMER 'Your brand X is dear, isn't it? It is only 45p down the road.'

The reply to this one can take one of three forms, depending on how much you value your customer and the price you are actually charging.

(1) If the price thrown at you is a lot cheaper than you can buy it for — 'Rubbish! I don't believe it. There must be something wrong with it. In fact I'll give you 50p for every packet you bring in to me.'

(2) If the price is not all that much cheaper, and you value your customer — 'They have probably got a special offer on it. We did it for 44p a few weeks ago.'

(3) If the price is not all that much cheaper, and you do not value your customer anyway —
'. . . well go down the road and buy it there, then!'

Mind you, if you do reply with number (3) above, the answer will sometimes surprise you, as in the following two instances:

(a) 'I would buy it down the road, but they have sold out.'
(b) 'I HAVE always bought it down the road, but they don't sell it any more!'

There's none so odd as people!

Starting a Christmas Club

Running a Christmas Club can be a very useful additional source of income, and should be actively encouraged, Not only will it boost your turnover by the amount collected during the year, but it will ensure that those customers will come into your shop at Christmas time to choose their goods and whilst there, spend money.

Christmas Clubs can be run in a variety of shops — grocers immediately spring to mind, but there is no reason why greengrocers, newsagents, off-licences, butchers, etc., cannot also benefit from running them.

There is no need to spend more than a minimal amount on stationery. Any exercise book will provide an adequate record of the customer's deposits. Begin by numbering the pages on the top corner, leaving the first two pages blank to write the names and page number allotted. When a deposit is made, turn to the appropriate page and enter the date, the amount of the deposit, and the signature of the person taking it. The same details are entered on the customer's card as a receipt. These cards may be purchased through your buying group or wholesaler if you use one, or may be ordered through a printer to your own design, or may simply consist of a piece of thin white card folded in half, with your stamp and the words 'CHRISTMAS CLUB' on the front. There are special Christmas Club stamps available, but I have always thought them to be an unnecessary expense.

Try to get as many people as possible to join the club immediately after Christmas, and notices strategically placed, especially by the till, will be beneficial.

It is best if you keep this money separate, apart from your own, so

64

Mrs Pellett

Date	Amount	Sign.	Date	Amount	Sign.	Date	Amount	Sign.
5/1/84	50p	H.E.	B/F			B/F		
12/1/84	£1	R.Lewis						
19/1/84	50p	R.Lewis						
22/1/84	£2	K.						
26/1/84	50p	H.E.						

as not to be tempted. A good idea is to buy premium bo.
hope for a bit of luck, or place it in a deposit account.
Towards the end of November, work your way through ᵥ
totalling all the payments, to save time later when the customers
to collect.

Insurance

Every shopkeeper tries to keep his overheads as low as possible, and it
is very tempting, when things are not going as well as they could, to
forego or reduce the insurance cover on the shop and contents. This is
false economy, and is definitely not recommended. It is no use having
the attitude — 'It could never happen to me', because by the law of
averages one day it will, and every day you spend in the shop is a day
nearer to that unahppy event. It is much better to make economies in
other directions, considering the relatively small amount of money
involved in premiums and to be able to sleep well at night. Your trade
depends to a certain extent, on your attitude towards your customers.
If you are worrying about the possibility of being robbed, or having
your windows smashed, in addition to all the other problems involved
in running a business, you will not be able to do yourself justice, and
may consequently suffer a loss in trade greater than the amount of the
insurance premium you have avoided paying, without even having any
losses.

Perhaps my own experience may be of help to you when weighing
up the pros and cons of insurance. From the time I bought my first
shop I have always been insured. I went for years without a mishap,
until 1968, when three men came into my newagent's shop/post office,
and whilst two of them kept my wife busy at the far end of the shop,
the third crept behind the counter, opened the till, grabbed the notes
and ran, closely followed by his two accomplices. We had in the region
of £70 taken, and were surprised by the promptness with which the
insurance company paid out.

After that we did not have another claim until 1979, when my
children broke the glass in the front door of our grocer's shop, whilst
larking around. Again we had a swift payment, this time through a
different insurance company. By the start of 1983 we had been paying
our insurance premiums regularly for years and years, with only those
two minor claims during that whole period. If ever anyone had any
doubts about the necessity of insurance, it was me.

In January I arrived at the shop early in the morning and found the
back window had been forced open, and the whole place was a
shambles. Thieves had broken in during the night, and had taken a till,
security cameras and monitor, and many items of stock, totalling in all
just over £2,000. the insurance company insisted on the window being
permanently sealed in future, and paid up.

Five weeks later, I was awakened at six o'clock in the morning by the sound of the telephone ringing. It was the police. "I have reason to believe that your shop has been broken into, sir,' the constable said. I hurriedly dressed and drove over to find that the constable's words must have been the understatement of the year. There were dents and scratches around the window, where the thieves had obviously tried, and failed, to enter. They had then turned their attention to the back door, and with a pickaxe or crowbar or similar, had ripped the back door and frame out of the wall, and again took over £2,000 worth of stock. This time the insurance company were not quite so quick at settling, but eventually we received the money. Incidentally, two weeks after the second break-in they were back again, but left empty-handed after not being able to get through the specially reinforced replacement door.

I am not saying that my case is typical, but it is true, and should be borne in mind if ever you are thinking of saving a few pennies at the expense of insurance.

Do not underinsure. If you do so, and you have a claim, you may come up against an ugly word called 'average'. I have never really understood *why* it should be so, but this is the way it works. If you have stock valued at £10,000, but only insure it for £5,000, and this stock is totally destroyed, the insurance company may only entertain a claim for £2,500, on the grounds that you are accepting half the risk yourself. It still seems cockeyed to me, but if you have an 'average' clause in your policy, make sure you are fully covered.

Types of Policy

The main types of policy are as follows:

Fire, Storm, Tempest, Flood and Explosion This is self-explanatory. The premium for this type of policy is usually about 25p per £100 insured.

Loss of Profits or Consequential Loss Insurance The idea of this insurance is to pay for fixed expenses such as rent, rates, telephone etc., which will still be due even if the shop is unable to open because of fire etc. The premium for this is usually about 30p per £100 insured. For an additional premium it may be possible to cover the cost of staff wages also.

Burglary Unfortunately, with the recent increase in the number of burglaries generally, insurance companies are finding this a very unremunerative part of their work, and are now usually insisting on both higher premiums, and the installation of alarm systems. The only good news is that modern technology has improved the quality and selection of alarm systems available, whilst also bringing down the price.

Employer's Liability This insurance is obligatory, and covers any claims against you from any of your employees who meet with an accident whilst on your property.

Public Liability If a member of the public is injured on your premises, this insurance will cover you. Judging by some of the awards that have been made to the public in the past, you would be well advised to effect this insurance, if nothing else.

Products' Liability This is to cover any claim made against you, that cannot be held to be the responsibility of the manufacturer.

Shops 'All-In' Comprehensive Policy Most shops are insured under one of these schemes, designed by various insurance companies, which gives production against most events. They usually cover the following: Fire, storm, tempest, flood, explosion, burglary, lightning, thunderbolt, subterranean fire, earthquake, housebreaking, riot, aircraft and other aerial devices, strike, civil commotion, labour disturbances, bursting and overflowing of water pipes, malicious persons, impact by road vehicles, and employer's liability.

If you wish to know which policy would be best for you, it is advisable to contact an insurance broker, who will have details from several companies, and who will not charge for his services, as he obtains his commission directly from the insurance company concerned. Some trade associations have arranged insurance 'packages' at preferential rates for their members, and if you belong to one of these groups it may be beneficial to enquire if one is available.

Points to Note

A few other points to look out for in policies are:

Seasonal Increases Most policies automatically increase the insured amounts during the Christmas period, but if your business varies greatly at other times of the year, perhaps due to a local festival, or tourism and holidaymakers, you may need to extend it to cover these periods.

Account Customers This is rather a difficult one, but what happens if all your books are destroyed in a fire and it is not possible to find out how much is owed to you by various people?

Automatic Reinstatement Find out if your policy provides for 'automatic reinstatement'. If it does not you may find yourself underinsured without realising it. For example, say you insure a certain class of goods for £1,000 and suffer a break-in, in which £800 worth are stolen, the insurance company will pay out, but will only insure afterwards for the balance, i.e. £200, unless there is an 'automatic reinstatement' clause.

Most insurers now allow business premiums to be paid by instalments for a small extra premium. It may be worth while enquiring if this is so with your insurance company.

If you have a problem resolving an insurance claim, you can complain to the British Insurance Association.

If you have a non-business insurance claim which is not settled agreeably by the insurance company, you may complain to The Insurance Ombudsman, Insurance Ombudsman Bureau, 31 Southampton Row, London WC1B 5HJ, telephone 01 404 0591. This service is only for UK policies taken out by individuals in their private capacity, and is therefore no use for a shop policy, but it may be used for a private car or household policy. In the case of a dispute the Ombudsman is required to make a fair decision which is binding on the insurance company, but which you can reject if you wish. The Bureau is subscribed to by the majority of insurance companies.

Inflation

Ask most people who are not in business, and some who are, 'What is the meaning of "Inflation is coming down"?'; and you will probably be given the answer 'Prices are meant to be coming down, but I can't see where', or words to that effect. 'Inflation is coming down' means '*The rate* of inflation is coming down', or the speed at which prices are increasing, is slowing down. They are still going up. But slower.

One of the problems with inflation is the fact that it costs more and more money to keep your stock levels the same. To illustrate this, if the stock on your shelves has cost you £5,000, and inflation is running riot at 20 per cent, next year it will cost you £6,000 to fill your shelves, and £7,200 the year after. If your profits do not increase proportionately, you are faced with the decision to either ask for an overdraft or reduce your stock. Either way you will be out of pocket, firstly from interest charges from the bank, and secondly from even more reduced sales because of your reduced stock.

Inflation is not new. It has been going on since pre-Roman times. In this country money had little importance before the Middle Ages, when an unskilled labourer earned ½p per day, and a prosperous farmer was able to live comfortably on £4 per year. Eggs cost 2p a 100, pears ½p for 36, a gallon of best ale cost ½p, *but* a pound of sugar cost just under 10p (three weeks wages for a labourer).

Prices rose slowly up to about 1520. Twenty years later they had almost doubled. By the time Elizabeth I came to the throne in 1558, prices were almost three times as high as they were 40 years earlier when her father Henry VIII was on the throne. At the end of the sixteenth century prices were four times as high as they were in 1500.

Prices doubled again in the first 50 years of the seventeenth century.

In 1550 a maid would earn £1 a year, and labourers 1½p a day. By 1600 the labourer was earning 3½–4p a day, and a loaf of bread cost 1½p. The total daily sales of an average shopkeeper were 20p. Best beef was around 1½p a pound, and sugar had gone down to 5p a pound.

A chicken cost ½p in 1515, 1p in 1603, and 6½p in 1650. And so on — cheese cost 1p a pound in 1750, beer was 1p a gallon, a pair of shoes cost about 15p, a farm labourer earned about 6p a day, a cook £8 a year, and there was a £40 reward for catching a highwayman. It cost 5p to have a tooth extracted.

By the mid-nineteenth century beef was 3p a pound, a haircut was a penny, a bottle of whisky was 16p, a cook earned £20 a year, and a doctor with a thriving practice £1,000 a year.

By 1935 a coalminer earned £3 a week, a bus driver £4 a week, a High Court Judge £100 a week. Milk was 1p a pint, cheese 3½p a pound, sugar 1p a pound, a Morris Oxford from £260, and so on
. . . . . .

All this may have nothing to do with running a shop — but it is good background knowledge, and I think it is interesting.

Resale Price Maintenance

RPM is the governing, by manufacturers, of the retail price of the goods they produce, and was almost universally followed until it was made unlawful in 1964 by the 'Resale Prices Act, 1964'. RPM is still operable on certain classes of goods, e.g. books, newspapers, drugs etc. If a company wishes to continue RPM on its goods, it must satisfy one of the following conditions:

(1) There will be a decline in the quality, number, or variety of particular goods.
(2) There will be a decline in the number of outlets selling the product.
(3) In the long term prices will increase.
(4) After-sales service, for goods which require it, will suffer.
(5) Goods will be sold in a manner as to be injurious to health.

If a retailer undercuts the price of one of the few remaining items still subject to RPM, he will probably be warned initially by the manufacturer, and then, if he still persists, may either have supplies terminated, or an injunction sought from a civil court to restrain him.

It may be of benefit to shopkeepers to understand more of the effects of the Act.

Many people believe that the abolition of retail Price Maintenance heralded the demise of the small trader. The public loved the idea, because it meant cheaper prices, more goods sold, and therefore more employment. Everyone would benefit, the public and manufacturers alike. Let us take a closer look, and see what has actually happened, and how everyone has 'benefited'.

(1) The Small Shopkeeper

This country used to be known as a nation of shopkeepers. The abolition of RPM sparked off a war which left thousands of shops dead, and many more thousands maimed, and becoming weaker every day. The small shopkeeper nowadays has to pay more to the manufacturer for many goods than the cut-price multiple is charging the public. He is continually accused of 'over-pricing' and making exhorbitant profits, by both the public and the media, even though more and more shops are closing down or going bankrupt each day. The small shopkeeper has definitely *not* benefited from the abolition of RPM.

(2) The Manufacturer

The manufacturing industry in this country is in a far from healthy state, with redundancies reaching all-time heights. If this is the current situation, bearing in mind the abolition of RPM, it makes you wonder what it would be like if it had stayed. Or does it?

(3) The Public

The public probably still believe they are better off. They accept what they are told, especially when it is written in a newspaper. Let us see how they have actually benefited.

(a) Wider Choice: In fact, the opposite has happened. How many times have you looked for a commonplace article in a large store, and been told they no longer stocked it? The policy of all the large stores is that if an item does not turn over 'x' number of times a year, it is delisted and not replaced. The selection of stock in a small specialist shop is, and always has been, much more comprehensive than that in a large multiple, because the proprietor of the small shop is not as concerned with stock turn, as he is with providing a full selection of goods.

(b) Easier Shopping: or 'One stop shopping' as it is called, is meant to make shopping easier, but because of (a) above, it either means buying substitute goods, or making another trip to find what you want.

(c) Better Trained Staff: They may be trained to take your money more quickly, and in a better manner, but, unfortunately, they generally have no knowledge of what they are selling, and even less of associated items. If you need any advice, you will be better off going to a specialist shop, and may even save money in the long run.

(d) Cheaper Prices: There is no question that the most popular widely advertised lines are sold cheaper in the multiple stores, and the public

is brainwashed into believing that this applies to all the goods. This is not true, as can be borne out by a survey you can carry out yourself. There is a very disturbing factor in all this. Multiples are able to sell the most popular lines at these cheap prices, because they have such buying power they can bargain with the manufacturer to supply on their own terms. This means that the price reductions are not offered by the multiple concerned, but by the manufacturer, and ultimately borne by the small shopkeeper who has to pay the full price. If this trend continues, many manufacturers will go to the wall because they will not be able to satisfy the demands of the multiples and still make a profit. This will result in an even smaller selection for the public, and eventually, when a few multiples control the market, prices will rise. This would then fulfil almost all the conditions at the start, which determined whether a class of goods sold should be exempt or not.

Surely, in the best interest of the public, it would be wise to reintroduce RPM, so that prices can *generally* go down, manufacturers can flourish, and everyone can find a job. After all, the government make it illegal to pay staff below a set wage, why not make it illegal to sell below a set price?

Off-Licences

One method of increasing your sales is by applying for an off-licence, so that you may sell intoxicating liquor, and take advantage of the peak drinking seasons of Christmas and hot summers. Before elaborating on the procedure for applying for a licence, it might be as well to look at the possible drawbacks involved.

(1) Your insurance premiums will be substantially increased.
(2) You will tie up a lot more money in stock.
(3) You will become more of a target for break-ins.
(4) If you do not have one already, your insurance company will probably insist on a burglar alarm system.
(5) If you intend selling half and quarter bottles of spirits, you will have to be constantly on the alert because of the vulnerability of these items to both customers and staff, bearing in mind the size and value.
(6) You will have to pay solicitors, advertising, and other costs, in order to apply for a licence, and then, if granted, a yearly licence fee.
(7) You will be expected to sell bottles of whisky and gin, and other top sellers, for virtually nil profit.

You will have to offset all of the above against the additional sales you hope to obtain from both the off-licence, and the customers it generates, bearing in mind the proximity and quality of the opposition. If you decide to go ahead after weighing up all the pros and cons, here is what you have to do:

(a) Brief your solicitor, if using one, and supply full details of the shop including the landlord if leasehold.
(b) Decide on the appropriate date for the hearing, bearing in mind the Clerk of the Justices needs all the relevant details 21 days beforehand.
(c) Prepare a plan of the shop, showing the intended sales and storage areas. A scale of 1:50 is recommended.
(d) Prepare a summary of the location (facilities, type of area, housing etc.).
(e) Prepare a map showing *all* licensed premises within at least ¼ mile. (You can check these at the office of the Clerk to the Licensing Justices, from the Licensing Registrar.)
(f) Formal notices of application must be displayed in the shop for 7 days during the 28 days prior to the hearing. (Supplied by your solicitor.)
(g) Three weeks before the hearing the police, local council, and fire authority should be notified. You can expect a visit from each of these at any time without prior notice.
(h) An advertisement must be placed in the local newspaper covering the area.

The following factors will be taken into account at the hearing:

(1) *Your past experience* — obviously you stand more chance if you have previously held a licence without having had any problems.
(2) *the location of your shop* — objections could be raised if the granting of a licence might possibly create any traffic congestion.
(3) *Objections from other people* — possibly neighbours, Licensed Victuallers Association, police, other off-licences etc.
(4) *Whether you are applying for a full spirit licence* — or just a beer, wine and cider licence.
(5) *You will have to prove* all relevant notices have been displayed and served.

If you are thinking of presenting your own case I strongly advise you to attend a transfer session first, to see exactly what is entailed. The following points should be borne in mind:

(1) First, and most importantly, you will have to show *need*. A petition is a good idea and should be run, and, if at all possible, two or three respectable witnesses should be brought to court on your behalf.
(2) You will have to show that you are a 'fit and proper' person to hold a licence, and that you will be in charge of all liquor sales.
(3) You will have to state your proposed opening hours.
(4) You will have to describe where the liquor will be stocked, and the security arrangements you intend to apply.

Costs Involved

If you present your own case it will obviously be cheaper. Professional fees vary a great deal. If you use a solicitor make sure he is experienced in licensing procedures, and has expert knowledge of these cases.

There will be the cost of advertising in the local paper. It may be that it will be necessary to advertise in more than one newspaper to ensure coverage of your area.

There will be the cost of the licence, if granted.

Renewal of licences is at the Brewsters Sessions held during the first two weeks of February each year. A renewal form is usually sent out, and should be returned within the specified time, but, remember that the Court is not obliged to send out reminders, and if you forget to renew, the licence lapses on 4 April, and a formal renewal must be applied for at the next transfer sessions. In this case it is a serious offence to carry on selling liquor.

Any retail sale of liquor, or any other goods for that matter, is entirely up to the discretion of the proprietor, and no reason for refusing a sale ever has to be given. No sales may be made to any person under 18 years of age, nor by any person under 18. It is an offence to allow customers to consume alcohol on the premises, which they have bought from your store. It is also an offence to sell drink to any person who is drunk or behaves in a riotous manner.

The permitted licensing hours must be strictly adhered to. These are:

Monday to Saturday: 8.30 a.m. to close of licensing hours for the district (normally 10.30 or 11.00 p.m.)
Sundays, Christmas Day and Good Friday: 12 noon to 2.00 p.m. and 7.30 p.m. until close of licensing hours for the district.

If you deliver, the following rules also apply:

(1) There must be no sale on credit. All liquor must be payed for in full in the shop during permitted hours.
(2) Details of the purchaser, and liquor to be delivered, must be entered into both a day book to be kept on the premises, and a delivery book to be carried by the person making the delivery.

If you wish to alter the position of your off-sales section within your shop, you should inform the Clerk to the Justices, and send a plan of the shop. If you are unable to obtain a Justices' Licence you may still sell beers, wines and spirits as long as you obtain a wholesale dealer's licence, and conform to the minimum wholesale quantities. These are as follows:

(1) Wines and spirits may be mixed, and must be either one case of 12 bottles containing between 68cl and 80cl, or at least 9 litres.

(2) Beer and cider should be in at least two case lots, or a minimum of 21 litres. A case consists of 24 cans each containing 440ml.

No individual bottles may be displayed or sold

Further information about a wholesale licence may be obtained from your local Customs and Excise Office.

The Other Side of the Coin

If you hold an off-licence and find an application has been made by a nearby competitor, the first thing you should do is to write to the Clerk to the Licensing Magistrate, setting out in as strongly worded a letter as possible, your reasons for opposing the application, stressing the fact that the needs of the public are already well catered for, and there is absolutely no necessity for another outlet. You should also attend the hearing in person, and state your reasons for objecting. Most importantly, take along a map of the area showing the existing stores, to prove the point.

Advertising

The short answer as to whether a shopkeeper should advertise or not, is 'no'. The only time it may pay off is if he is offering something that is different, or cannot be obtained from the local shops. It would be pointless for a newsagent to advertise the quality of his chocolates, or a greengrocer his oranges, or a grocer his selection of jams. It would not draw much more response if they advertised how cheap they are on those items, because the public is used to seeing special offers on these goods every time they go shopping. It might be worth while for a speciality range, such as a grocer selling free range eggs and goats' milk, or a camera shop, or a hobby shop, or something similar. Specialist shops such as stamp dealers, coin dealers, etc. find that a lot of their business comes from advertising in magazines concerned with these goods, and will draw from a much larger area, but for the ordinary 'bread and butter' shop, newspaper advertising will not produce sufficient extra sales to warrant the expense. It would be far better in these cases to have some leaflets printed, promoting your goods, and including a special offer or two, and then having them distributed locally on a door-to-door basis by a firm of leaflet distributors, or arranging something with a local newsagent. Of course, if you have a newsagency, your costs will be minimised by slipping the leaflets into each newspaper.

With regard to advertising in local school programmes, church magazines etc., spend what you can afford, or what you would like to donate to the organisation, but do not expect to get any return from them.

Advertising is a legitimate business expense, and goes against tax. If your type of trade is such that newspaper advertising still appeals, or you fancy doing it anyway, then it is generally accepted that the best places to be, if you can, are on the front page, the back page, or the right-hand side of page three (this has nothing to do with the *Sun*). If you wish to advertise for some weeks book on a period rate, rather than a week-to-week basis, because substantial savings may be made in this manner. Obviously you will advertise in the most widely read local newspaper, which may not be the one with the largest circulation. Ask your local newsagent which paper is most popular in his shop, and choose that one. You may find that its rival is more popular in a neighbouring town which has a larger population, and hence a greater circulation. It will probably be of negligible benefit to advertise elsewhere than in your own locality. As a rule of thumb, it is generally better to spread your financial commitment over a long period, rather than have one big splash. 'Little but often' is the motto. If you are contemplating having a very special offer, it might be worth while finding out about local radio advertising. If you are opening a new business it might also be beneficial to enquire about having a well-known personality to open the shop.

Trade directories are a waste of time for the ordinary shop, because no housewife is going to look through such a publication in order to find where her nearest butcher or baker is situated. For specialised businesses, the Post Office 'Yellow Pages' is sufficient, in which a display or semi-display advertisement is much preferred. Other forms of advertising to be considered are the local cinema, which is not as expensive as one might imagine, buses, tubes, trains and advertisement hoardings.

At some time or another you will be asked by an advertising salesman to take space in some sort of local directory or advertising campaign. Check into the venture as much as possible and *on no account hand over any cash* even if you are offered a discount. A large proportion of these are never published.

Free Advertising

This is not as impossible as it sounds. Local newspapers are always on the look out for stories that might be of interest to their readers, and any items of news which are about the neighbourhood shopkeeper will receive an attentive ear. If anything out of the ordinary happens in or around the shop, or to you, or a member of your staff, it is well worth a telephone call to the local papers. They may send along a reporter and photographer to cover the story, and provide you with far better publicity than any advertisement you care to make up. And it is free. If they say 'no', it has cost you nothing but a telephone call. I have benefited from this several times in the past, and now give a couple of examples of how it can be done.

Once we bought a post office that had been closed for three months, and was next door to a grocer's shop we already owned. The local reporter arrived to obtain a background story, and whilst talking, I mentioned in passing that I belonged to a particular society. The following day the reporter returned with a photographer, and the resultant article and photograph appeared on the front page of the next edition, informing everyone of the re-opening of the post office, and making great play of the society I was a member of, and extolling the home-cooked hams, free range eggs, and selection of bacon, I offered in the grocer's. Marvellous advertising.

The same thing happened on other occasions after winning various trade competitions, and even after winning a competition that had nothing to do with shops at all.

The Best Advertisement of All

This costs you nothing but hard work and being pleasant. It will come from your shop itself, from the clean, inviting image on the outside, to the pleasant friendly service, and good stock range on the inside. This is self-perpetuating advertising, and takes advantage of the customer at the best possible time, i.e. when she is there. She does not have to remember to visit a particular store when next she is in the vicinity, nor to have to make a special journey when she does not really want to. She is already outside the shop and does not need a lot of encouragement to be enticed in.

Another form of advertising is to have the name of your shop displayed on the side of a van. This is a two-pronged weapon however, because although the image is beneficial on a spotlessly clean shiny van, it can be detrimental if the van is allowed to get dirty, rusty, or sport a few dents. Also the manner in which the van is driven will have an effect. If it is raced around the district, causing chaos and annoyance, it will do much more harm than good, by causing present and potential customers to swear as much about your shop as your van.

Be Your Own PR Man

Success in publicising a company, whether large or small, is achieved not by chance, but by effort. Huge companies have special public relations departments whose sole job it is, is to issue press releases and photographs, and to arrange press conferences, exhibitions, displays, television and radio spots, and anything else which will advance the name, products, and prestige of their company.

Obviously you cannot expect to get the same coverage yourself, but by being constantly aware that you are the PR man for your own business, you should be able to make full use of any local news that concerns yourself or your business, by copying the methods of the professional PR man.

Press Releases

These should be headed 'Press Release', be typewritten on a single page, and should tell your story in as few words as possible. Try to emphasise the local interest aspect as much as possible, and end the report by saying 'For further information contact . . . , on [give telephone number]'. Send copies to all the local newspapers.

If any of the papers are interested in your story, they may send along a reporter to interview you, or your staff, and you should make sure you are available for this. On the other hand, they may ask you to write a feature article on the subject.

If a reporter does come to visit you, there is no need to lay down the red carpet and provide a running buffet, although a cup of coffee would probably not come amiss once the throats begin to dry.

Press releases should be prepared and sent at the earliest opportunity, to try and beat any publishing deadlines of the paper concerned.

Photographs A photograph will always add interest to a press release, and if one is enclosed if should have a description on the back for easy reference purposes. Sharp, glossy, black and white prints, no larger than half plate (6½″ × 4¼″) size, are ideal. If the prints are not yet ready, but will be available shortly, a note to that effect should be enclosed.

Local Radio and Television Press releases can be sent to local radio and TV stations in exactly the same manner as above, but the chances of them being used, are naturally very much slimmer.

If you are fortunate enough to be featured in an editorial, do not be persuaded to place an advertisement alongside it. This will ruin the effect completely, and will leave the reader wondering whether the original story is part of the advertisement, and may then question the credibility of it. It would be far better to take advertising space in the next issue, and enjoy two weeks advertising for the price of one.

Being your own PR man means greeting your customers with a friendly cheerful smile, encouraging your staff to do the same (they will take their lead from you — misery is just as infectious as laughter), and being able to ensure that your bank manager has confidence in you. Cultivate these assets and you will not go far wrong.

Bear in mind that some events that seem commonplace to you, may be of interest to the local paper. It is therefore worth taking a fresh look at everything around you, or perhaps even manipulating events slightly to encourage the press to take a closer look.

Looking After Your Health

Your health is your most precious asset. It is absolutely pointless driving yourself to the brink of exhaustion by working 12 hours a day, six or more days a week, in order to try and amass a fortune, and then drop down dead in the attempt. On the other hand, if your business needs to open for those hours just to cover the expenses and make a small profit, without being able to pay for staff, your best bet is to get out as fast as you can, and either look for something more profitable, or go out and get a job, where you will probably work half the hours, have four weeks paid holiday a year, no worries, and earn more.

Long hours can quite easily be worked for a time when you are young and energetic. For the space of 18 months, when I was not quite 30 years old, I owned a 'Bake'n'Take' next door to our newsagent's. I started work at six o'clock in the morning marking up newspapers, and finished at about half past eleven at night in the Bake'n'Take, six days a week, and seven o'clock to one o'clock on Sundays. By the end of the year and half, lumps had started to break out on my face, and I was told by my doctor that I was thoroughly run down. As there was not sufficient turnover in the Bake'n'Take to enable it to be completely staff-run and still show a decent profit, I sold it immediately, and my health returned. I would not dream of doing those hours again.

Food presents the next problem for many shopkeepers. It is all too easy to fall into the trap of not eating at all during the day, or rushing out to the back of the shop, bolting down a couple of sandwiches, and returning to serve within the space of two minutes. Whether the result of a prolonged spell of this brings on chronic indigestion or ulcers depends on your physical make-up, but you would be well advised for both your health and sanity, to have at least 45 minutes off at lunch time, either by arranging staff hours to provide this, or by closing the shop. Again, if you are not busy enough to employ staff, you are not going to miss much in the way of takings and profit if you do close.

The other problem with food usually comes when you own a food shop. It is very easy, especially when you sell many tempting, fattening foods, such as cream doughnuts, chocolates, and ice cream, to continually nibble or sample during the day, and end up obese. You then stand a very good chance of getting a coronary. A careful watch should be kept on your weight, and if it shows signs of a relentless gradual increase, you must go on a diet. I have suffered from this problem over and over again during the past many years, and eventually designed a means of dieting which suited me best. Incidentally, I enlarged this to form a book called *Healthy Slimming* which I thoroughly recommend to anyone who suffers from the same problem.

Exercise or the lack of it, is the next area to watch. You may think that you get sufficient exercise in the shop, running backwards and forwards, but I strongly suggest that you make a point of going for walks, or playing golf, or doing anything that is different to your daily routine, especially if you live above the shop. Many shopkeepers lead a very narrow and confined life, caused through spending all their time, both working and leisure, in the shop. This can only lead to a deterioration in both mental and physical health, especially if the type of trade you are in allows you to spend most of the day sitting down.

Selling your Wares

Finally in this part some thoughts on possibly the most important aspect of your business.

Shelf Fillers or Salesmen.

Do you employ 'shelf fillers' or 'salesmen'? Many many potential sales are lost everyday whenever a customer enquires about a product from a salesman, and finds they are answered by a shelf filler. Some people are natural salesmen. The rest of us have to learn the technique of salesmanship, and it is *your* job to turn your shelf fillers into more productive units for your own benefit.

Customer's Motives for Buying

Making a sale, regardless of the product involved, depends on that product appealing to the customer's needs. Sales staff have to determine firstly what that need is, and then concentrate on satisfying it, rather than trying to sell the product alone. The *customer's motives* for buying can be classified under the following headings:

Getting a Bargain Most people cannot resist getting a bargain, whether it be 30 per cent extra, 3 for the price of 2, or a price that appears to be far below that normally charged.

Comfort Price usually plays a secondary position here. The main object is to find out exactly what usage the article will be put to. For instance, it would be futile trying to sell a comfortable armchair to someone who needs a chair to sit at a desk, or trying to sell someone a Rolls-Royce because they asked to see something a little more comfortable than a Mini.

Health Sell the benefits, not the flavour. In other words, people will eat the most vile-tasting rubbish if they believe it will make them more virile/beautiful etc.

Pride Keeping up with the Joneses may be an old-fashioned expression, but it is still as applicable today as ever. In fact nowadays, with modern technological advances, the name of the game should be 'keeping ahead of the Joneses'. Whether it be cars, computers, videos or any of the other luxuries that are now taken for granted, the latest models will certainly enhance the ego, even if the additional facilities do not enhance the products. Pride of course, only applies to products that will be seen by others. This is why the food trade generally does not try to appeal to customers on these grounds, and is one reason why the majority of shoppers choose inferior quality 'own brands' — they know these items will not be seen by others. There are two instances that do occur however, which involve pride. The first is when food or drink is offered to guests, and the second is when shopping at a fashionable store, for example, Harrods, or Fortnum and Mason.

Personal Attraction Perfume, after-shave, cosmetics and clothing come within this category. Think how the TV adverts portray the effects of using their after-shave. No man really believes that *every* woman will become jelly in his hands when he is wearing it, but . . . ?

The 'Impulse' Sale These are usually sales made from the siting and display of goods, and may be 'impulse' sales. For instance, pension book holders will sell steadily if placed by a post office counter, cheap digital watches and calculators sell when displayed on a petrol station pay counter, and confectionery goods sell when placed by a till. On the other hand a quick display of sunglasses in a prominent position on a bright sunny day will pay dividends, as will umbrellas and wellington boots when it is raining, and cough and cold sweets and cures when the weather favours them.

Of course, to be able to sell the goods properly, the salesman must have the confidence of the customer, and this will only come if the salesman shows sufficient knowledge of the product he is selling. Therefore staff should be made aware of all new trends, and be encouraged to read the trade press, as well as keeping an eye on the opposition whenever the opportunity arises.

The Sale — In Six Easy Stages

A completed sale is comprised of various steps, unless the customer knows exactly what he or she wants — type of goods, make, model and price. The stages should be memorised so that a smooth sale ensues leading to a satisfactory conclusion. They are:

(1) *The Greeting* The customer should be approached in a friendly manner, and *always* with a smile.

(2) *The Inquiry and Motive* Tact is the keyword here. The salesman should establish what type of goods are required, and if possible *discover the motive*.

(3) *Presenting the Article* Each possible choice should be shown to the customer, pointing out all the selling points, and linking them to the *buying motive*.

(4) *Selecting a Short List* From the above selection, a short list should be obtained after discounting those items which are too cheap, too dear, wrong colour, wrong size, etc. If possible allow the customer to handle the goods, and immediately remove any that have been discarded, so that the ultimate choice does not become confusing.

(5) *Advising* If a customer is unsure either about buying at all, or deciding between various models, the salesman should recommend one make, reassuring the customer of the quality, service, guarantee, etc., and again linking to the *buying motive*.

(6) *Closing* The hardest part of any sale, whether you are selling a box of chocolates, a television, a suite of furniture, a car, or central heating, is 'the close'. Closing the sale means finishing the transaction; commending the customer on his good taste; taking his money; and leaving him with a feeling of satisfaction. As soon as the customer has made a choice, start to finish the transaction by wrapping the goods, or writing out a sales invoice. Do not carry on talking about it, or dithering, because the longer the delay, the more chance there is that he may change his mind.

Trading Stamps

Trading stamps are used to breed some form of loyalty amongst customers and as an incentive to make them use your shop in preference to that of a competitor. Many stamp companies have come and gone over the years, and extreme caution should be exercised before committing yourself in any way. Understand fully that not only will it be very difficult to stop giving stamps if takings do not come up to expectations, but that you could have a lot of irate customers on your hands if the stamp company goes bust.

The best known company in this field is Green Shield Stamps which was relaunched in 1987 after ceasing to trade in the seventies due to a combination of rapid inflation and the loss of Tesco as a main customer.

Their stamps are in books of 5000 which cost approximately £29.00 each. One stamp is given for each 25p spent in the shop, therefore each book has a retail value of £1250. The stamps cost roughly 2% of your turnover. To work out how much extra you need to take in the shop to cover the cost, deduct 2% from your gross profit %, and divide this figure into your actual gross profit, then multiply by 100.

EXAMPLE: Takings £2000 @ 17% = £340 GP
              340/15 × 100 = £2266

Any takings over £2266 per week will be at *15%* GP.

Don't forget to take account of your staff. They will take longer to complete a transaction, and there will always be a temptation for them to give 'extras' to their friends and themselves. They would probably not even think of it as stealing.

There is another way of testing the water, which in some circumstances may be beneficial, and which has the advantage of being able to be stopped at any time with no ill effects. That is to do it all yourself.

You will have to have your own vouchers printed. Give one with each complete 50p or £1 spent in the shop and display a range of goods with voucher values beside each. You can run this promotion initially for a couple of months to see the reaction, and then either scrap it or continue for a further period. Or you could even go on to trading stamps!

PART 4

Looking Ahead

Subletting Flats above Shops

For those of you who do not live, or propose not to live, in the accommodation above a shop, I know how frustrated you probably feel about it. You have a potential source of additional income, which unfortunately contains certain drawbacks. The biggest of these drawbacks is that if you find a suitable tenant, and later decide to sell the business, the value of the business will be reduced because of the sitting tenant. If you decide to ignore this fact and go ahead, your first step must be to obtain the landlord's permission, be they private individuals, companies, or councils.

Many leases contain clauses that preclude this, by insisting that the accommodation is occupied only by the lessee, a member of his family, or a full-time shop employee, but there is nothing to stop you approaching the landlords again in this respect. If the answer is again 'no', then that is the end of the matter, because if you go ahead regardless, you will be in breach of your lease, and could face serious consequences. You may run the risk of losing all your money in the event of being forced to sell your business because of ill health or some other reason, and then finding that you are being evicted for 'informally' letting the flat. You will then have no business to sell.

Assuming you obtain permission you have various choices:

(1) Unfurnished Letting This is obviously the easiest way. There are no planning consents needed, and you will be inundated with prospective tenants. The big drawback is, that with current legislation it will be practically impossible to get them out, and if you decide to sell the business you will probably lose at least as much as you have earned because of the sitting tenant, especially if you sell quickly.

(2) Furnished Letting This has the disadvantage that it costs money to furnish a flat with adequate furniture, utensils, and cooking facilities, and although financially in the long term the prospects are good, in the short term it may be inconvenient because of the cost. Vacant

possession may be obtained by letting for a specified period only, and then giving notice.

(3) Service Letting This is one way of offering a little more to a manager, and keeping the accommodation occupied. The written statement of terms and conditions which is given to the manager should state that the arrangement is a 'service' occupation, to avoid any arguments later.

A service letting is one where the property is occupied primarily for the interests of the proprietor, to ensure the shop is open in time in the mornings, has some degree of protection at night, for general emergencies, and to enable the manager to carry out his duties to the best of his abilities. It must not be let out to an employee with the prime motivation of obtaining rent, because the situation then could result in a normal tenant/landlord relationship, and end up with a sitting tenant.

If a manager, who is enjoying the benefit of a service tenancy, finds other employment, he must vacate the premises immediately, so that his employer is able to employ another manager under similar terms.

(4) Office Accommodation This is possibly the best way of all. Unfortunately, you need planning permission for this, and local authorities are very loath to grant it, as they say it takes away from the residential accommodation available which is not in the general interest whilst there is a housing shortage.

(5) Student Lettings This is worth looking into if you have a polytechnic or university near you, and are willing to take a chance on wild parties etc. It will of course only be during term time.

Staying, Selling or Expanding?

After a certain length of time, depending on your nature and when any outstanding loans are due to be completed, you will no doubt look at your current lifestyle and financial position, and consider your future anew. You basically have three choices:

(1) To stay where you are, as you are, for the foreseeable future.

If you have been in the same shop for a few years, you will no doubt have made new friends and aquaintances, as will your children, if you have any. You may also be involved in local activities and have a very rosy social future. All these things must be weighed against how the shop is actually performing — its current trend. You have made a substantial investment in the shop, and as long as your takings and profits increase in line with inflation you will be able to continue with no worries. However, if your takings have dropped due to factors which will not resolve themselves in the near future, you must have a serious think, because, apart from your capital investment dwindling in real terms, you will probably end up by taking a continuously decreasing wage and working longer hours. If you feel you cannot bear to leave your friends, or the niche you have carved for yourselves, it might be a good idea to give serious thought to selling the business, buying a house instead, and both partners going out to work for the same number of hours previously worked in the shop. At least that way, you will have no problems about being sick or having holidays!

(2) To stay where you are and buy another shop.

This situation will usually occur either when your shop has been trading fairly successfully for some time, and you want to expand but not move, or when a good opportunity presents itself in the neighbourhood.

It is very easy to become euphoric over this, and I would be the last to dissuade anyone from going ahead, but great care and thought should be given to various areas, such as:

Staff Your wage bill will be much higher, particularly if you yourself are working in your present shop at the moment, because you will need to find a replacement for those hours to enable you to concentrate on making both shops pay, and to give sufficient time to the increased amount of bookwork involved.

Shopfittings and Equipment if you are not buying a going concern, make sure of *all* your initial costings, for viability.

Loss of Trade You should assume in your costings, that there will be a loss of trade in your present shop, and if the shop you are buying is an owner-occupied going concern, a loss of trade there also. If this does not happen, count it as a bonus.

Buying Terms Although by buying larger quantities you may receive larger discounts, do not include these in your costings, because they may be swallowed up by increased pilferage through your not being able to exercise the same level of control as at present.

(3) To move to a larger shop

This is a natural progression, the economics of which have been fully covered in Part 1.

Having decided to sell, you are now faced with two immediate problems.

1. Do you buy first, or sell first?
2. Do you use an agent, or try to sell yourself?

Buy first or sell first? The answer will depend on the type of business you are looking for, and the locality. If either of these is very specialised, for example a greengrocer's taking over £15,000 a week, or a particular level of trade in a confined area, you will do better to wait for that shop to come on the market, and then put yours up for sale, because it could take quite a long time. You will probably have to pay top price for the business as well, unless you are very fortunate.

In all other cases I advise sell first, and although you should have been looking at particulars of businesses for sale for some time, do not actually visit any to look over, until you find a buyer for your own. This will make life a lot easier, and save any hassle or pressure put on you if you happen to see a shop that you like.

Agents: To use, or not to use? The first few shops I sold were through agents, and I had no real complaints. Their advantages are that they advertise regularly, have a register of applicants, and form an important liaison during the sale between vendor, purchaser and their respective solicitors.

Their two main disadvantages are their fees — generally about 3–6 per cent of the price realised, not including stock, and the fact that once they have found a buyer for your shop, they put off anyone else who may be interested. This means that in the event of your purchaser withdrawing or delaying after four or five weeks, you have no option but to start completely from scratch.

The last couple of shops I advertised and sold myself, and was utterly amazed at how easy it was. The main advantages, of course, are that you save yourself the agent's fee, and you have a list of interested parties who you can contact yourself at any time if trouble appears imminent. The choice, as always, is yours. If you decide to use an agent, it may be an idea to try and get a reduced commission rate by offering a sole agency for say, a month. If after this time you have not found a buyer, spread it around and be prepared to wait or reduce your price. Or you can advertise it yourself also.

Pricing Whether you use an agent or not, you will have to decide on the lowest acceptable price *to you*. Only you know what this is. It depends how badly you want to get out. Be realistic. Comparative prices can be obtained fairly easily from looking through *Dalton's Weekly* or your trade magazine. Add on a few thousand, taking into account agent's fees if applicable, and be prepared to take an offer. Nobody likes paying the full price, regardless of how cheap that price may be. Everybody likes to think they are getting a bargain.

Advertising Your trade magazine or *Dalton's Weekly*, or both, are your best bets. Make your advert stand out and be sufficiently large to be noticed. Mention *all* the good points, and none of the rest. Run it for four weeks. You will probably find that you get most response from the second week, with the third and fourth not far behind.

As an example, in 1983 I advertised a grocer's shop for one week in the *Grocer*, and for the three following weeks in *Dalton's Weekly*. I had 10 replies from the *Grocer*, 9 from the first week in *Dalton's*, 19 from the second week, and 12 from the third week. And these were all from box numbers!

Box Numbers The *advantages* of using a box number are that you will not get people telephoning or popping into the shop unexpectedly and asking the staff "Is the shop still for sale?" It will stop a lot of the local nosey parkers, because when they write for details they will have to reveal their names and addresses. You then have the option of seeing them, or replying that the shop has now been sold, but that you will get back to them if any problem arises. You do not have to give your address. You will also have a complete list of the correct names and addresses of everyone who replies.

The *disadvantages* are that you will not get as good a response as if you advertised the address of the shop, or the telephone number.

Showing People Over Your Shop Make appointments for times that are convenient for yourself. If a prospective purchaser is not willing to fit in with them, he is not very serious. Make a note of the names and addresses and times of each viewer, and write alongside a description of them and their comments. Do not be in a hurry to accept any offer which is not sufficient if you still have other people to see, or there are other people interested. Once you have agreed on a price, ask for a preliminary deposit to be sent to your solicitor.

One point must be mentioned at this stage. There has recently been an increased number of break-ins following shops being put on the market. It would seem that this provides prospective thieves with an ideal opportunity to 'case the joint', and see if there is anything worth stealing. This applies equally to 'viewings' arranged through agents, as to those from your own adverts. There is nothing to stop any thief telephoning an agent and arranging an appointment to view. The answer is to have as small a display of valuable stock as possible, to ensure the doors and windows look impregnable, and to talk vaguely about the burglar alarm. It does not matter if you do not have one — they will not know. At least if you are unfortunate enough to have a break-in following your shop being put on the market, and advertised by yourself through a box number, you will have a complete record of every person you sent details to, and a description of everyone who came to view.

Make sure your accounts are right up to date, and you have photocopies of these to hand out to interested parties.

After you have accepted an offer your solicitor should prepare and send a draft contract to the purchaser's solicitor as soon as possible, and the landlord should be informed to find out what references will be required. Very shortly afterwards you will be visited by the landlord's surveyor, and will then receive a Schedule of Dilapidations. This is when you are held over a barrel by the landlord, because until this Schedule has been completed to his satisfaction, he will not sign the Licence to Assign, and you are stuck. However, if you have looked after the property, the Schedule may only consist of a couple of minor repairs or replacements. From then on it is a matter of keeping your fingers crossed that all goes well.

PART 5

The Shopkeeper and the Law

Introduction

If there is one thing sure in this world, it is that the number of rules and regulations affecting the employer, and the rights of his employees, will continue to grow virtually every year. You are therefore strongly advised to check the current position with the relevant authority before taking any action whatsoever. The following notes are intended for guidance purposes only, and do not purport to be an authoritative legal interpretation.

This section provides a guide to the legislation that has been brought in during the past twenty years, and which affects the shopkeeper. The provisions are now contained mainly in the Employment Protection (Consolidation) Act 1978, as amended by the Employment Acts 1980 and 1982, and should be noted well, because no matter how good the relationship is between employer and employee, friction can arise at any time in the future over any issue, and it is as well to know the law, and not be made to look a fool by arguing erroneously.

Personnel

Written Statement of Main Terms and Conditions of Employment

This was introduced in order to give all employees certain minimum rights as to conditions of employment, and those laid down by the 1978 Act are only minimum terms. There is nothing to prevent the employer and employee from agreeing better terms between themselves in a contract of employment.

A contract of employment exists as soon as an employee proves his or her acceptance of an employer's terms and conditions of employment by starting work, and both employer and employee are bound by the terms offered and agreed. Unless there is already in existence a written contract of employment containing all the necessary details,

149

the employer must give to the employee, not later than 13 weeks after
he has started work, a written statement of the main terms of
employment, including a note on disciplinary and grievance procedures, and entitlement to a period of notice. The provision does not
cover:

(1) Anyone who is not an employee, for example an independent
    contractor.
(2) Employees who normally work less than sixteen hours per week,
    unless they have been employed continuously by their employer
    for at least eight hours a week for at least five years.
(3) Employees whose written contracts of employment already cover
    the matters in question, provided they are notified about disciplin-
    ary and grievance procedures.

The Written Statement must contain certain particulars and an
additional note on disciplinary and grievance procedures. It must
contain the following:

(a) The name of the employer.
(b) The name of the employee.
(c) The date when the employment began, and whether any employ-
    ment with a previous employer counts as part of the continuous
    period of employment with him, and if so, the date on which the
    continuous period of employment began.

The statement then has to give the following particulars of the terms
of employment at a specified date not more than a week before the
statement is given to the employer.

(d) The scale, or rate of renumeration, or the method of calculating
    renumeration.
(e) The intervals at which renumeration is paid, that is whether weekly
    or monthly or some other period.
(f) Any terms and conditions relating to hours of work (including
    normal working hours).
(g) Entitlement to holidays, including public holidays, and holiday
    pay (sufficient to enable the employee's entitlement, including any
    entitlement to accrued holiday pay on the termination of employ-
    ment, to be precisely calculated).
(h) Terms and conditions relating to incapacity to work due to
    sickness or injury, including any provisions for sick pay.
(i) Details of any pensions or pension schemes in operation.
(j) The length of notice of termination which the employee is obliged
    to give and entitled to receive, or, if the contract is for a fixed term,
    the date when the contract expires.
(k) The title of the job which the employee is employed to do.

Sometimes contracts of employment have no agreed terms under one or more of these headings. For each item, when there are no particulars to be given, the written statement must say so. The written statement must contain an additional note. This note must:

(l) Specify any disciplinary rules (other than those relating to health and safety at work) which apply to the employee, or must refer to a document, reasonably accessible to the employee, which specifies the rules.
(m) Specify, by description or name, the person to whom the employee can apply and the manner in which an application should be made, if dissatisfied with any disciplinary decision relating to him or her, or for the purpose of seeking redress of any grievance relating to his or her employment.
(n) Explain what further steps, if any, follow from an application.
(o) State whether a contracting-out certificate under the Social Security Pensions Act 1975 is in force for the employment in respect of which the written statement is being issued.

For all or any of the particulars and information listed above, the written statement may refer employees to a document or documents which they have reasonable opportunity to read in the course of their employment, or which are made reasonably accessible to them in some other way. Documents which might be used in this way include wages regulation orders, and sick pay schemes.

If there is a change in the terms, the employer has to inform the employee about it within one month of its introduction by means of a further written statement covering the change, unless the employer's obligation is met by keeping reference documents up to date. An employer who makes use of reference documents may give a written undertaking that they will be kept up to date. Changes in the terms in question do not then have to be notified through further written statements, but the reference documents must be brought up to date within a month of each change.

Change of Employer

A new statement is not required if the employer's identity is retained but the name is changed, or if a change in the identity of the employer does not break the continuity of employment, (see below). Provided that there is no other change in the terms of employment, a new employer need only notify the employee in writing, within one month, of the change in the name or identity of the employer, spcifying the date on which the employee's continuous period of employment began.

Continuity of employment is preserved if:

(a) A business is transferred to another employer.
(b) Under an Act of Parliament one corporate body takes over from another as the employer.
(c) The employer dies and his or her personal representatives or trustees keep the employee on in employment.
(d) There is a change in the partners, personal representatives, or trustees who employ the employee.
(e) The employee moves from one employer to another where at the time of the move the two employers are associated employers.

If there is any dispute regarding the implementation of the Act, both the employer and the employee have the right to refer the details to an industrial tribunal. The Department of Employment will advise on the procedure for this, if necessary.

It may be beneficial to include in the written statement the fact that hours may possibly have to be reduced if necessary, or you may be forced to pay redundancy for 'constructive dismissal'.

Also, the risks of staff pilferage can be reduced by making it a condition of employment that staff must be prepared to be stopped at any time to have their possessions or persons searched. Without this provision an employer is not legally entitled to make a search.

Itemised Pay Statement

Under employment protection legislation, employees who normally work sixteen hours or more a week are entitled to be given an itemised pay statement for their wages or salary. Every pay statement must give the following particulars.

(1) The gross amount of the wages or salary.
(2) The amounts of any fixed deductions and the purposes for which they are made.
(3) The amounts of any variable deducations and the purposes for which they are made.
(4) The net amount of wages or salary payable.
(5) The amount and method of each part payment when different parts of the net amount are paid in different ways.

Example of Written Statement

DATE .... EMPLOYEE ....

EMPLOYER ....

● Your employment began on .... and employment with your previous employer did not count as part of your continuous period of employment.

● Your employment began on .... and as your previous employment with .... counts as part of your continuous period of employment, this is deemed to have begun on:

....

TITLE OF JOB

PAY   INTERVALS OF PAY

HOURS OF WORK

HOLIDAY ENTITLEMENT

SICKNESS or INJURY

PENSIONS & SCHEMES

RIGHTS TO NOTICE By employer ....

                          By employee ....

FIXED CONTRACTS

DISCIPLINARY RULES – If you are dissatisfied with any disciplinary decision you should raise it orally/in writing with:

....

GRIEVANCE PROCEDURE – If you have any grievance relating to your employment you should raise it orally/in writing with:

....

A contracting-out certificate is/is not in force for the employment in respect of which this statement is given.

Any changes in terms mentioned above will be notified within one month, and the office record is available for inspection.

Rights of the Expectant Mother

The maternity provisions set out in the various Employment Acts are quite involved, and if this event does arise, it is suggested a visit to the local Employment Office for fuller details would be well worthwhile. The main points are as follows:

(a) Any employee who is pregnant and who, on advice, attends a clinic or other place of antenatal care, has the right not to be unreasonably refused time off work to do so, and to be paid for the permitted time off.

(b) An employee who fulfils the qualifying conditions for Statutory Maternity Pay is entitled to return to her original job at any time before the end of the period of 29 weeks, beginning with the week in which her baby was born, subject to notice being given in writing.

(c) If the employer employed five or fewer employees immediately before the start of her maternity absence, and it is not reasonably practicable to reinstate her in her original job or to offer her suitable alternative employment, it will not be regarded as a dismissal.

Transfer of a Business or Undertaking

The Transfer of Undertakings (Protection of Employment) Regulations 1981 apply to the transfer of a business or undertaking, or as a part of it, to a new employer (for example, through the sale of a business or part of it). It provides for the following:

(a) Any employees who are employed by the old employer at the time of the transfer automatically become the employees of the new employer as if their contracts of employment were originally made with the new employer.

(b) The new employer takes over all the employment liabilities of the old employer (except criminal liabilities and occupational pension rights).

(c) If either the old or the new employer dismisses an employee solely or mainly because a business or part of a business has been transferred, the dismissal will be considered unfair.

(d) However, if a dismissal, either by the old or the new employer, is necessary for economic, technical or organisational reasons associated with the transfer, it may be considered fair if a tribunal finds that this is the main reason for dismissal and if it also finds that the employer acted reasonably in treating this reason as sufficient to justify dismissal.

Notice of Termination of Employment

The Act gives the right both to employer and employee of a minimum period of notice of termination of employment. If a contract of employment gives the employer or the employee rights to longer notice than the minimum in the Act, then the longer period of notice applies.

The Act does not prevent either employers or employees from waiving their rights to notice or from accepting a payment in lieu of notice. Nor does the Act affect the right of either party to terminate the contract without notice if the conduct of the other justifies it.

The minimum periods of notice do not apply to the following:

(1) Employees who normally work less than 16 hours a week, unless they have been employed continuously by their employer for at least eight hours a week for at least five years.

(2) Anyone who is not an employee, for example an independent contractor.

(3) Most employees who have fixed term contracts.

The periods of notice required to be given if an employer wishes to terminate a contract of employment with an employee who has been employed for a continuous period of four weeks or more, are:

(a) At least one week's notice if the employee has been employed continuously by th.. employer for less than two years.

(b) If the employee has been in continuous employment with the employer for a period of between two and 11 years exclusively — a minimum of one week's notice is required for each year worked.

(c) If the employee has been in continuous employment with the employer for 12 years or more — a minimum of 12 weeks notice is required.

An employee is required to give the employer at least one week's notice if employed continuously for one month or more by that employer. This minimum is unaffected by longer service.

Written Reasons For Dismissal

Employees who have been dismissed, and have completed at least six months continuous employment before the effective date of termination, may, by request to their employer, orally or in writing, obtain a written statement of the reasons for dismissal. A request must be met within 14 days. This does not apply to employees who do not qualify for notice of termination.

Dismissal

Dismissal is defined as the termination of employment by:

(1) The employer, with or without notice.

(2) The employee's resignation, with or without notice, because of

certain conduct of the employer (known as 'constructive dismissal').
(3) The expiry of a fixed term contract without its renewal.
(4) The employer's refusal to allow an employee to return to work
after the birth of her baby where she has a legal right to do so.

The following is also classed as being 'fair' or 'unfair'.
The following people cannot complain of *unfair* dismissal.

(1) Those who are not employees (for example, an independent
contractor or freelance agent).
(2) Employees who have not completed two years continuous
employment with their employer at their effective date of
termination
(3) Employees who normally work less than 16 hours a week unless
they have been employed continuously by their employer for at
least eight hours a week for at least five years.
(4) Employees who before their effective date of termination had
reached the normal retirement age for their employment or, if
there is no normal retiring age, had reached age 65 for men or 60
for women.
(5) Certain employees with fixed term contracts.

Dismissal of an employee can only be *fair* if the employer can show
that the reason for it was one of those listed below, and provided that
the employer acted reasonably in the particular circumstances.

(1) A reason related to the employee's conduct.
(2) A reason related to the employee's capability or qualification for
the job.
(3) Redundancy (broadly, this is where the employer's need for
employees to do certain work has ceased or diminished or is
expected to do so).
(4) A statutory duty or restriction on either the employer or the
employee which prevents the employment being continued.
(5) Some other substantial reason which could justify the dismissal.

Acting reasonably with regard to each of the above, means:

(1) *Misconduct:* A new recruit should have the duties of the
employment fully explained, and should know what actions are
considered so serious that a first offence means summary dismissal,
that is dismissal without notice or pay in lieu of notice. Except where
the default is so serious as to justify summary dismissal, for example
where an employee has been caught 'red-handed' in an act of gross
misconduct, an employee should always be told in what way he or she
is at fault and warned that an improvement must be made. It is not
essential to put warnings in writing, but it is desirable to do so. The

employee should be given a reasonable time to improve after being warned.

(2) *Inability to do the Job:* The new employee should have been given adequate training, including guidance on the methods of work required, and on standards of performance expected. He or she should have had proper supervision, been told of any shortcomings, and been given a chance to improve.

(3) *Redundancy:* Victims should not be selected through personal prejudice and been given as much warning as possible. Fair grounds for the choice of redundancy may be length of service, or a combination of factors such as service, skill, work performance, and attendance.

(4) *Legal Barriers:* If the continued employment of someone in a particular job would result in the law being broken, that person can be fairly dismissed. An example of this is when someone who is employed to drive loses his or her licence.

(5) *Some Other Substantial Reason* such as:

(a) difficult staff relationship.
(b) changed duties or conditions which were not acceptable to the employee.
(c) false details on an application form.
(d) business reorganisation.
(e) inability to retain a replacement worker after the return of the original employee. The dismissal itself must still be carried out in a reasonable manner with proper explanation and due warning.

Redundancy Pay

Under the 1978 Act, employers are required to make a lump sum compensation payment, called a 'redundancy payment', to employees dismissed because of redundancy. The amount of the payment is related to the employee's age, length of continuous service with the employer, and weekly pay up to a maximum (£158 a week from 1 April 1987 but subject to annual review). The employer must also give the employee a written statement showing how the payment has been calculated, at or before the time the redundancy payment is made.

Employees who have not completed two years continuous employment, generally with the same employer, or who have reached age 65 for men or 60 for women, have no entitlement to redundancy payment. Service under age 18 does not count, and the maximum length of service used in calculating redundancy payments is 20 years.

If you employ 9 or fewer employees you are able to claim part of the cost of redundancy payments (currently 35%) from the Redundancy Fund, and forms on which to claim this rebate are obtainable from redundancy payments offices of the Department of Employment. The Redundancy Fund is financed by an allocation from the Class 1 National Insurance contributions paid under the Social Security Act 1975 by employers and employees; such contributions are earnings related. If you employ 10 or more staff, whether part time or full time, there is NO rebate.

Where the employer is genuinely unable to make the required redundancy payments, for example because of insolvency or financial difficulty, the employer should contact the local Redundancy Payments Office of the Department of Employment and explain the situation. It may then be possible for the redundancy payments to be made from the Redundancy Fund, and that part for which the employer is liable recovered at a later date.

There was a case recently where the purchaser of a business was told by the vendor that he employed no staff, only family. When the business actually changed hands the new owner was most upset to learn that there *had* been an employee, and that she wished to continue working for the new owner. Because of financial pressures, there was no way in which the employee's wages could be met, and she then asked for her redundancy money, although she had never worked for the new owners, and was unknown to them. An Industrial Tribunal decided she was entitled to redundancy pay, and the new owners had to comply. The onus is on the purchaser to make a proper investigation into the affairs of the business and ascertain actual staffing levels.

There is a ready reckoner for redundancy payments on page 159.

Ready Reckoner for Redundancy Payments

The ready reckoner for redundancy payments shown below has minor deviations for certain ages and lengths of service, but in most cases may be taken as being accurate.

Length of Service

Age	2	3	4	5	6	7	8	9	10	11	12	13	14	15	16	17	18	19	20
20		1	1	1	–														
21	1	1½	1½	1½	1½	–													
22	1	1½	2	2	2	2	–												
23	1	2	2½	3	3	3	3	–											
24	1½	2½	3	3½	4	4	4	4	–										
25	2	3	3½	4	4½	5	5	5	5	–									
26	2	3	4	4½	5	5½	6	6	6	6	–								
27	2	3	4	5	5½	6	6½	7	7	7	7	–							
28	2	3	4	5	6	6½	7	7½	8	8	8	8	–						
29	2	3	4	5	6	7	7½	8	8½	9	9	9	9	–					
30	2	3	4	5	6	7	8	8½	9	9½	10	10	10	10	–				
31	2	3	4	5	6	7	8	9	9½	10	10½	11	11	11	11	–			
32	2	3	4	5	6	7	8	9	10	10½	11	11½	12	12	12	12	–		
33	2	3	4	5	6	7	8	9	10	11	11½	12	12½	13	13	13	13	–	
34	2	3	4	5	6	7	8	9	10	11	12	12½	13	13½	14	14	14	14	–
35	2	3	4	5	6	7	8	9	10	11	12	13	13½	14	14½	15	15	15	15
36	2	3	4	5	6	7	8	9	10	11	12	13	14	14½	15	15½	16	16	16
37	2	3	4	5	6	7	8	9	10	11	12	13	14	15	15½	16	16½	17	17
38	2	3	4	5	6	7	8	9	10	11	12	13	14	15	16	16½	17	17½	18
39	2	3	4	5	6	7	8	9	10	11	12	13	14	15	16	17	17½	18	18½
40	2	3	4	5	6	7	8	9	10	11	12	13	14	15	16	17	18	18½	19
41	2	3	4	5	6	7	8	9	10	11	12	13	14	15	16	17	18	19	19½
42	2	3½	4½	5½	6½	7½	8½	9½	10½	11½	12½	13½	14½	15½	16½	17½	18½	19½	20½
43	2	4	5	6	7	8	9	10	11	12	13	14	15	16	17	18	19	20	21
44	2½	4½	5½	6½	7½	8½	9½	10½	11½	12½	13½	14½	15½	16½	17½	18½	19½	20½	21½
45	3	4½	6	7	8	9	10	11	12	13	14	15	16	17	18	19	20	21	22
46	3	4½	6	7½	8½	9½	10½	11½	12½	13½	14½	15½	16½	17½	18½	19½	20½	21½	22½
47	3	4½	6	7½	9	10	11	12	13	14	15	16	17	18	19	20	21	22	23
48	3	4½	6	7½	9	10½	11½	12½	13½	14½	15½	16½	17½	18½	19½	20½	21½	22½	23½
49	3	4½	6	7½	9	10½	12	13	14	15	16	17	18	19	20	21	22	23	24
50	3	4½	6	7½	9	10½	12	13½	14½	15½	16½	17½	18½	19½	20½	21½	22½	23½	24½
51	3	4½	6	7½	9	10½	12	13½	15	16	17	18	19	20	21	22	23	24	25
52	3	4½	6	7½	9	10½	12	13½	15	16½	17½	18½	19½	20½	21½	22½	23½	24½	25½
53	3	4½	6	7½	9	10½	12	13½	15	16½	18	19	20	21	22	23	24	25	26
54	3	4½	6	7½	9	10½	12	13½	15	16½	18	19½	20½	21½	22½	23½	24½	25½	26½
55	3	4½	6	7½	9	10½	12	13½	15	16½	18	19½	21	22	23	24	25	26	27
56	3	4½	6	7½	9	10½	12	13½	15	16½	18	19½	21	22½	23½	24½	25½	26½	27½
57	3	4½	6	7½	9	10½	12	13½	15	16½	18	19½	21	22½	24	25	26	27	28
58	3	4½	6	7½	9	10½	12	13½	15	16½	18	19½	21	22½	24	25½	26½	27½	28½
59	3	4½	6	7½	9	10½	12	13½	15	16½	18	19½	21	22½	24	25½	27	28	29
60	3	4½	6	7½	9	10½	12	13½	15	16½	18	19½	21	22½	24	25½	27	28½	29½
61	3	4½	6	7½	9	10½	12	13½	15	16½	18	19½	21	22½	24	25½	27	28½	30
62	3	4½	6	7½	9	10½	12	13½	15	16½	18	19½	21	22½	24	25½	27	28½	30
63	3	4½	6	7½	9	10½	12	13½	15	16½	18	19½	21	22½	24	25½	27	28½	30
64	3	4½	6	7½	9	10½	12	13½	15	16½	18	19½	21	22½	24	25½	27	28½	30

Men Only

To use the table: Read off the employee's age and number of complete years service. Any week which began before the employee attained the age of 18 does not count. The table will then show *how many weeks' pay* the employee is entitled to.

Anti-Discrimination Legislation

This legislation is very complicated, and full details of the provisions of the Acts may be found in two guides *Sex Discrimination* and *Racial Discrimination*, published by the Home Office and available free of charge from Job Centres and Employment Offices. The main points are:

Sex and Race: Under the Sex Discrimination Act 1975, it is unlawful for employers to discriminate on grounds of sex or against married persons. The Race Relations Act 1976 outlaws discrimination by employers on racial grounds, that is on the grounds of race, colour, nationality (including citizenship) or ethnic or national origins. For the purposes of both Acts, discrimination is less favourable treatment of someone on the specified grounds. It also includes applying requirements or conditions which, though applied equally to all, have a disproportionately detrimental effect on particular groups or a particular sex (as the case may be) and which cannot be shown to be justifiable (for instance, to be job related).

Equal Pay

Employers are required to afford equal treatment in terms and conditions of employment to men and women who are employed on 'like work' or work related as equivalent under a job evaluation study. Equal pay is, therefore not restricted to renumeration alone, but includes all terms of a contract of employment other than those relating to death or retirement.

Food Labelling Law

This law came into effect on 1 January 1984, and is intended to make food labelling as uniform as possible throughout the Common Market. It applies to all types of foods, but particularly to manufactured prepacked items. Fortunately the onus for this is on the manufacturer. If you sell fresh non-prepacked foods you are obliged by the new regulations to display the country of origin, the grade or class, the name of the food and the variety, and the price per pound or unit.

Statutory Sick Pay (SSP)

Statutory Sick Pay (SSP) was introduced in the Social Security and Housing Benefits Act 1982, and was later amended by the Health and Social Security Act 1984, and then by the Social Security Act 1985. Under this Act employers became responsible for yet another complex piece of legislation — that of paying sick pay to their employees for up to 28 weeks at a time. SSP is treated like wages in that it is subject to PAYE income tax, and to National Insurance contributions.

Employers are able to recover the gross amount of any SSP they pay plus their share of the National Insurance contributions due, by holding back an appropriate amount from the National Insurance and PAYE payments they send each month to the Inland Revenue. SSP is payable to all employees who are sick for four or more days in a row, except for those in the following categories:

(1) Employees who are over State pension age on the first day of sickness (65 for men, 60 for women).

(2) Employees who have been taken on for a specified period of no more than three months.

(3) Employees who have average weekly earnings less than the lower weekly earnings limit for National Insurance contribution liability.

(4) An employee who has done no work for you under the contract of service.

(5) An expectant mother who is off sick during the time starting 11 weeks before her expected week of confinement and ending six weeks after. (See Statutory Maternity Pay.)

(6) An employee who has already been due 28 weeks SSP from his previous employer.

(7) An employee who has a gap of 56 calendar days or less between the end of a State benefit claim and the start of a PIW.

(8) An employee who is in legal custody.

If your employee is in one of the above groups and is sick, you are required by law to complete an 'exclusion form' SSP1(E) and give or send it to him so that he may claim State sickness benefit instead.

A Day of Sickness for SSP is a day on which the employee is incapable, because of a specific disease or disablement, of doing work he can reasonably be expected to do for you under the contract of service. Only complete days of sickness can count for SSP.

PIW or 'period of incapacity for work' is a spell of four or more days of sickness in a row (Sundays and Public Holidays included). There is no SSP liability for less than four days sickness, and no action need be taken.

Qualifying Days are days on which the employee would normally have worked, had he not been sick. (It is possible to have any pattern of qualifying days, with the agreement of the employee, as long as there is at least one in every week, and they do not always have to be normal working days.) Also Qualifying Days must not be defined by reference to the days of your employee's sickness.

You do not pay SSP for the first three qualifying days in the PIW. These are called 'waiting days'. So you do not pay until the fourth qualifying day in the PIW.

Two or more PIWs (spells of sickness lasting at least 4 days) which are separated by 8 weeks (56 calendar days) or less are said to be 'linked' and are counted as one linked PIW. There are tables in the National Insurance contributions and SSP rates tables to help you work out if PIWs link.

You can ask your employee to produce any reasonable evidence in support of his entitlement, e.g. a self-certificate for spells of 4 to 7 calendar days, or a doctor's statement for spells of more than 7 days.

You can set your own rules about notification of sickness absence, within certain limits. Notification can be required orally, e.g. by telephone, or in writing or both.

You must make full details of your rules available to your employees. If an employer makes no rules, or his rules do not fall within the set limits, then an employee who notifies that employer of his sickness in writing no later than the seventh calendar day after a qualifying day of absence will satisfy the SSP requirements for that day.

Notification of absence does not mean EVIDENCE of sickness. You cannot require your employee to notify you of his absence by means of a doctor's certificate, but you can ask for one as evidence of incapacity if your employee is sick for more than seven days.

If an employee is late in notifying sickness for one or more qualifying days, and you are not satisfied that he had a good reason for his lateness, then you can if you wish, withhold SSP for the same number of qualifying days.

There are two weekly rates of SSP. Which one is paid depends on your employee's average earnings in the eight weeks before the sickness begins. The daily rate of SSP is the appropriate weekly rate divided by the number of qualifying days in that week. There is no SSP payable to employees whose average earnings are below the lower weekly earnings limit for National Insurance contribution liability.

The rates of SSP payable change each 6 April, and are included in current National Insurance tables. The rates for 1987/88 tax year are as follows:

£47.20 where earnings are £76.50 average per week or more.
£32.85 for average earnings of £39.00 to £76.49 per week.
Less than £39.00 — NO SSP payable.

If an employee leaves your employment within 8 weeks of a PIW you

will have to give him a leaver's statement, form SSP(L), w
by the DHSS.

You Are Required By Law To Keep The Following Record

(1) Dates of sickness absence of at least four consecutiv.
(including Saturdays and Sundays) reported by your employe.
(2) Any days within such sickness, absences for which SSP was N⌣r
paid, with reasons.
(3) Details of each employee's qualifying days in each PIW.
(4) Any leaver's statements given to you by employees who you did
not exclude from SSP.
(5) Copies of any leaver's statements issued by you.

These records should be kept in such a way that DHSS inspectors can
have access to them on request. You must be able to produce them
within a reasonable time if you are asked to do so, and must also keep
them for at least three years after the end of the tax year to which they
relate. You are also required by law to keep records showing, for each
pay day and each employee, any SSP paid as well as the usual records
of pay, PAYE income tax, and National Insurance contributions. You
can use the official Deductions working sheet or your own pay records
for this. The DHSS has produced an SSP record sheet, form SSP2,
available free of charge from local social security offices. It is not
compulsory to use it, but it will help in keeping the required records,
and is useful for working out what SSP is due.

The penalties for not complying with the regulations or trying to
falisfy records are quite severe, ranging up to a fine not exceeding
£2,000, or a term of imprisonment not exceeding three months, or
both.

Statutory Maternity Pay (SMP)

From 6th April 1987 employers must pay Statutory Maternity Pay
(SMP) to employees who satisfy certain conditions, the most
important of which is to be pregnant. (In the face of more and more
complex legislation being heaped upon the small businessman, some
light relief is necessary now and again). SMP is very complicated and
advice should be sought. The easiest solution, of course, is to only
employ women at a rate under the National Insurance contribution
level, or, if you have to employ them full time — make sure they are
sterilised!

To qualify for SMP an employee must fulfil each of the following
conditions:

(a) She must have been continuously employed by you for at least 26
weeks continuing into the 15th week before her baby is due. The
15th week is known as the Qualifying Week (QW).

(b) She must have average weekly earnings of not less than the lower earnings limit for the payment of National Insurance contributions which applies in the QW.

(c) She must still be pregnant at the 11th week before her expected week of confinement, or have been confined by that time.

(d) She must have stopped working for you.

(e) She must have notified you at least 21 days before her absence from work is due to begin, unless you decide to accept a shorter time.

(f) She will have to produce, within an acceptable period, medical evidence showing the date the baby is due on. This should normally be no later than the end of the third week of the Maternity Pay period.

SMP is payable for a maximum of 18 weeks.

There are two rates of SMP. A higher rate and a lower rate.

To qualify for the HIGHER RATE an employee must have either:

(a) been employed by you, normally working for at least 16 hours weekly, for a continuous period of 2 years up to and including the qualifying week, OR

(b) been employed by you, normally working for at least 8 but less than 16 hours weekly for a continuous period of 5 years up to and including the qualifying week.

The higher rate is $\frac{9}{10}$ths (90%) of the employee's average weekly earnings (based on the last eight weeks), and is payable for the first 6 weeks SMP is due. The lower rate is paid for the remainder of the period.

The LOWER RATE is a set rate which is reviewed each year. For the tax year 1987/88 the rate is £32.85 per week. There is no daily rate of SMP. If an employee qualifies for SMP, but not for the higher rate, she will be due the lower rate throughout the period of payment.

You can get back all of the SMP payments, including tax and NIC, by deducting these amounts from the monthly payments to the Collector of Taxes, in the same way as SSP.

Even if the employee is not going to return to work for you after the baby is born, you will still have to pay SMP for 18 weeks.

If the employee does not qualify for SMP, she can still get maternity allowance direct from the DHSS.

You Must Keep The Following Records:

(a) Dates of maternity absence notified by your employees.

(b) A record of any weeks within the period when SMP was not paid, and the reasons.

(c) Any maternity certificate or medical evidence given to you.

(d) Copies of any maternity certificate where the originals have been returned to the employee.

These records must be kept in such a manner that DHSS inspectors can have access to them on request. You must keep them for at least three years after the end of the tax year to which they relate. The DHSS has produced an SMP record sheet (form SMP.2) which is available from social security offices. It is not compulsory to use this form.

The penalties for not complying with the regulations or trying to falsify records are similar to those for SSP — ranging up to a fine not exceeding £2,000, or a term of imprisonment not exceeding three months, or both.

Health and Hygiene

The Food Hygiene Regulations affect anyone owning, managing, or carrying on a 'food business'. A food business is one in which food is sold or supplied for human consumption, whether or not run for profit. The Regulations themselves are available from HMSO or booksellers, and are enforced by the Local Authority Health Department, who will be glad to give advice on any aspect of food hygiene.

Any person who handles food is affected. The term 'handling' covers any operation in which food is involved, including the cleaning of equipment with which food comes into contact. Some requirements apply only to 'open food'. 'Open' food means food which is not in a container or completely sealed. The Regulations cover the premises, the protection of food from contamination, and personal hygiene and health.

(1) The Premises

These should be clean and in good condition, so that food cannot be contaminated directly or indirectly.

Ceilings: should not harbour dirt, and must be easily cleanable.
Walls: should be durable, smooth, impervious, washable, and of a light-coloured finish.
Floors: should be impervious without cracks or open joints, hardwearing and capable of being easily cleaned.
Doors, Stairs, and Windows: all joinery should be of simple design and finished with a hard gloss finish. Fingerplates and kicking plates to doors are an advantage.
*Fittings and Equipment:*should be constructed of smooth, readily cleansable, durable material. Open joints should be avoided. Equipment should be moved or so located that it can be readily cleaned on all sides and underneath.
Ventilation: adequate ventilation is to be provided to all areas. Ventilation canopies to be fitted over cooking ranges, chip fryers, etc.
Lighting: adequate natural and artificial lighting must be provided to all areas.

Vermin Proofing: food premises must be designed and constructed so as to prevent any risk of infestation by rodents and insects.
Pipework: where possible all pipework should be chased into the walls or ceilings and should not be boxed in. If pipework cannot be chased in then it should be positioned away from the walls and floors so that easy cleaning can take place.

You should provide the following:

(a) *Water Supply.* There must be a sufficient supply of clean water. If open food is handled, sufficient hot water must be available at each wash hand basin and at each sink.

(b) *Sanitary Conveniences.* These must be kept clean, in working order, well lighted and ventilated. Those used by food handlers must have a 'Wash Your Hands' notice visible. (These are available from the Health Education Council or your local Health Officer.)

(c) *Washing Arrangements.* All food premises must have enough wash basins in places where food handlers can get at them quickly and easily from their work place, and from the sanitary conveniences. Soap, nail brushes, and clean towels or paper towels must be provided at the wash basin. Basins must be kept clean and in good working order.

(d) *First Aid Kit.* Enough bandages, dressing, antiseptics etc. must be provided where food handlers can get to them easily. Outer dressings should be waterproof.

(e) *Clothing.* All clothing and footwear not used at work should either be kept in a locker or cupboard, or in a room in which food is not handled.

(f) *Equipment Washing.* Where open food is handled there should be sufficient sinks for washing food and equipment. The sinks must be kept clean and in working order, and be large enough to take the largest dishes and equipment comfortably.

(g) *Equipment.* All articles or equipment with which food may come into contact must be kept clean, in good condition, and as far as is practicable, be made from non-absorbent materals.

(h) *Waste Disposal.* Enough space must be provided in a suitable part of the premises for storing unsound food away from sound.

(j) *Covering Open Food.* Open food put out for sale will need to be covered if any risk of contamination is likely.

YOU MUST NOT

(a) Locate sanitary conveniences in a food room, or in a room which opens directly into a food room where open food is handled, or where odours can penetrate into a food room.

(b) Use a food room as a sleeping place. If a room opens directly into a bedroom, it must not be used for handling open food.

(c) Leave refuse or filth to accumulate in a food room.
(d) Send food for preparation or packing by outworkers in their own homes.

(2) The Protection of Food From Contamination

The rapid cooling of foodstuffs is essential. Unless they are about to be served or put out for sale, they *must not* be kept between the temperatures of 50°F and 145°F, or 10°C and 62.7°C. They must be kept really hot or really cool.

YOU MUST

(a) Keep cooked food and raw food apart. Working surfaces, knives, etc. are areas where contamination may occur.
(b) Keep food at least 18 inches above the ground, unless protected against contamination.
(c) Keep live animals and poultry away from food.
(d) Keep open food that is for sale, covered, whenever it is sensible to do so, to avoid contamination.

YOU MUST NOT

(a) Place food, or allow employees to place food, where there is any risk of contamination.
(b) Pack food in any material, paper, or container, which is not clean, or which might lead to contamination.
(c) Carry food in a container along with any article which may contaminate it.
(d) Keep animal feed in a food room unless it is in a closed container.
(e) Use, or allow anyone to use, the personal washing facilities for any purpose other than personal cleanliness.

(3) Personal Hygiene and Health

The rules with regard to these are as follows:

(a) You must keep your hands, face and other parts of your body likely to come into contact with food, clean at all times, washing hands frequently. Avoid touching your nose and lips whilst handling food.
(b) All clothing must be kept clean.
(c) Any cuts or grazes must be completely covered with a waterproof dressing.
(d) You must not spit.
(e) You must not smoke, chew tobacco or use snuff while handling 'open' food, or in a room where there is such food.
(f) You must notify the Medical Officer of Health of any occurrence of typhoid fever, or any salmonella infection, or dysentry, or any

other type of infection likely to cause food poisoning.

A point to bear in mind: if you sell open food, you cannot pass the buck. For instance, if you sell a sandwich in which there is mould, even though you have only just taken the bread from a freshly delivered loaf, you will be responsible and face possible prosecution, *not the baker.*

Shops Act

The Shops Act contains many conditions of employment for staff, the main ones being — for shop assistants of 18 years of age and over:

(1) They may not be employed for more than six hours without an interval of at least 20 minutes.

(2) If the hours of employment include a period from 11.30 a.m. to 2.30 p.m. an interval of not less than three-quarters of an hour (if they eat on the premises), or one hour (if their meal is not taken in the shop building), must be allowed.

(3) If the hours of employment include the period of 4 p.m. to 7 p.m., an interval of not less than half an hour must be allowed during that period.

(4) These provisions do not apply to a shop if the only persons employed as shop assistants are members of the occupier's family.

Persons under the age of 18 may not be employed for more than five hours without an interval of at least 20 minutes.

The regulations which apply to young persons under the age of 16 differ from area to area, and enquiries should be made from your Local Authority.

Sunday Trading

The laws concerning Sunday Trading contain many anomalies, and have been the subject of repeated attempts over the years to remove all restrictions. A list of 'allowable' goods and services is printed below. If, by chance the regulations have been abolished by the time you read this, it may have some curiosity value.

A shop may open on Sunday for the following purposes:

(1) The Sale Of:

(a) intoxicating liquors.

(b) meals or refreshments whether or not for consumption at the shop at which they are sold, but not including the sale of fried fish and chips at a fried fish and chip shop.

(c) newly cooked provisions and cooked or partly cooked tripe.

(d) table waters, sweets, chocolates, sugar confectionery and ice cream (including wafers and edible containers).

(e) flowers, fruit and vegetables (including mushrooms) other than tinned or bottled fruit or vegetables.

(f) milk and cream not including tinned or dried milk or cream, but including clotted cream whether sold in tins or otherwise.

(g) medicines and medical and surgical appliances at any premises registered under Section 12 or the Pharmacy and Poisons Act 1933.

(h) aircraft, motor, or cycle supplies or accessories.

(i) tobacco and smoker's requisites.

(j) newspapers, periodicals, and magazines.

(k) books and stationery from the bookstalls of such terminal and main line railway or omnibus stations, or at such aerodromes as may be approved by the Secretary of State.

(l) guide books, postcards etc. at any gallery, museum, garden etc. under the control of a public authority, or with the consent of the local authority.

(m) photographs for passports.

(n) requisites for any game or sport at any place where that game is carried on.

(o) fodder for horses, mules, ponies and donkeys at any farm, stables, hotel or inn.

(2) The Transaction Of:

(a) post office business.

(b) the business carried on by a funeral undertaker.

(3) A Few Other Transactions, being:

(a) The supply of goods to a club for the purposes of the club.

(b) The supply of goods required in case of illness.

(c) Attendance by a barber or hairdresser upon any person in an hotel or club who is resident therein.

(d) The sale of the products of his handicraft at his home, by a person to whom the local authority have granted a certificate of exemption.

(e) The sale by fishermen (elsewhere than in a shop) of freshly caught fish.

(f) The sale at a farm, smallholding etc. of produce, produced thereon.

(g) Sales on sea-going ships.

Offices, Shops & Railway Premises Act 1963

The Act applies to all offices and shops where people are employed, as well as other parts of the premises such as stairs, passages, landings, storerooms, exits, and yards. Several of the requirements are similar to the Health and Hygiene regulations. The main requirements of the Act which affect shops are as follows:

Main Requirements

(1.) *Cleanliness* All premises, fixtures, fittings, and furnishings must be kept in a clean state. No dirt or refuse must be allowed to accumulate, and floors and steps must be cleaned not less than once a week by washing, or if it is effective and suitable, by sweeping or some other method.

(2) *Temperature*

(a) Provision must be made for ensuring that a reasonable temperature can be maintained in every room in which people are employed to work otherwise than for short periods. For rooms where a substantial proportion of the work does not involve severe physical effort, a 'reasonable temperature' shall be not less than 16°C, or 60°F, after the first hour.

(b) This minimum standard of temperature is not required in rooms or shop premises where its maintenance is not reasonably practicable or would cause deterioration of goods. In these cases, employees must have access to means of warming themselves and the employer must give them reasonable opportunities to do so.

(c) A thermometer must be provided in a conspicuous place, so that employees may check the temperature of any room in which a 'reasonable temperature' has to be maintained.

(3) *Ventilation* In all workrooms there must be effective and suitable means of ventilation.

(4) *Lighting* There must be provision for suitable and sufficient lighting, either natural or artificial, in all parts of the premises. Windows and skylights must be kept clean.

(5) *Sanitary Conveniences* Sufficient and suitable conveniences must be provided. They must be kept clean and properly maintained, with effective lighting and ventilation. They must be conveniently accessible to the workers.

One closet is sufficient where either:

(a) the number of people employed to work in the premises does not regularly exceed five at any one time (whether or not both men and women are employed),

(b) each of the regular employees normally works in the premises for only two hours daily or less.

In all other cases separate sanitory accommodation must be provided for persons of each sex, and marked to show for which sex it is provided. Details of actual numbers of closets in proportion to employees may be obtained by reference to the Regulations.

(6) *Washing Facilities* Suitable and sufficient washing facilities must be provided, including a suitable supply of clean, running hot and cold water or clean, running warm water, and soap and clean towels or other suitable means of cleaning or drying. The place where they are provided must have effective lighting, and be kept clean and properly maintained. One wash basin is sufficient where the number of employees is as in 5(a) and (b). Where larger numbers of workers are employed reference should be made to the Regulations.

(7) *Drinking Water* An adequate supply of wholesome drinking water must be provided. If not piped, the water must be kept in suitable containers, renewed at least daily and preserved from contamination. Drinking vessels must be supplied, and there must also be facilities for rinsing them in clean water.

(8) *Accommodation for Clothing* Arrangements must be made for clothing not worn during working hours, and also for working clothes not taken home, to be hung up or otherwise accommodated.

(9) *Seating Arrangements* Where employees have, while working, reasonable opportunities for sitting without detriment to their work, a sufficient number of conveniently accessible seats must be provided at suitable places for their use. The employer must allow his workers to use the seats provided for them whenever this does not interfere with their work.

(10) *Eating Facilities* Where persons employed in shops eat meals on the premises, suitable and sufficient facilities must be provided for them to do so.

(11) *Floors, Passages and Stairs* All floors, steps, stairs, passages, and gangways must be soundly constructed and properly maintained, and so far as is reasonably practicable, kept free from obstruction and slippery substances.

(12) *Fencing and Exposed Parts of Machinery* All dangerous parts of machinery must be securely fenced unless they are so placed or constructed as to be as safe as if they were so fenced.

(13) *Cleaning of Machinery* No person under 18 years of age may clean any machinery if this exposes him to risk of injury from a moving part of that or any adjacent machinery.

(14) *Training and Supervision of Persons Working at Dangerous Machinery.* No person may work at any machine specified by the Secretary of State as dangerous unless he has been fully instructed as to the dangers and the precautions to be observed, and either has received sufficient training in work at the machine or is under adequate supervision by an experienced person.

(15) *Prohibition of Heavy Work* No person may be required, in the course of his work, to lift, carry or move a load so heavy as to be likely to cause him injury.

(16) *First Aid* A first-aid box or cupboard, containing only first-aid requisites, must be provided for the use of employees in all premises and must be readily accessible. The following items are required, (minimum quantities vary according to the kind of premises and numbers employed):

sterilised unmedicated dressings, assorted adhesive wound dressings, triangular bandages, adhesive plaster, cotton wool, sterilised eye pads, safety pins and (except where not more than ten persons are employed) a rubber or pressure bandage.

(17) *Fire Precautions* The following precautions must be observed in all premises:

(a) There must be such means of escape in case of fire as may reasonably be necessary in the particular premises.

(b) While employees are working or taking a meal on the premises, the doors through which they may have to pass to get out of the premises must not be so locked or fastened that they cannot be reasonably opened from the inside.

(c) The contents of rooms must be so arranged as to afford free passageway to a means of escape in case of fire.

(d) There must be appropriate fire-fighting equipment, properly maintained and readily available for use.

Accidents at Work

The Reporting of Injuries, Diseases and Dangerous Occurrences Regulations 1985 (RIDDOR) came into force on 1 April 1986.

Under these regulations you are obliged to report any of the following occurrences to the local office of the enforcing authority, as soon as you can, by telephone if possible:

(a) any accident causing death or major injury to one of your employees;

(b) any accident which occurs on premises which are under your control causing death or major injury to a self-employed person,

or a person receiving training for employment, or to a member of
the public;
(c) any notifiable dangerous disease;
(d) all injuries resulting from injuries at work which cause incapacity
for more than three days;
(e) the death of an employee if this occurs some time after a reportable
injury which led to that employee's death, but not more than one
year afterwards.

'Major Injury' is any injury which will result in the person injured
being admitted into hospital as an in-patient for more than 24 hours,
unless that person is detained only for observation.

Report these incidents immediately to the enforcing authority of the
Health and Safety Executive, which for retail shops is the local
authority. The notification should be made to the Environmental
Health Department of the authority in whose area the accident or
danger occurs.

Within seven days send a written report, on the new form F2508
(available from HMSO), to your enforcing authority.

You must keep a record of all reportable injuries and dangerous
occurrences, stating the following:

(a) the date and time of the accident causing the injury or of the
dangerous occurrence;
(b) the following particulars about the person affected:
(1) Full name. (2) Occupation. (3) Nature of injury or condition;
(c) place where the accident or dangerous occurrence happened;
(d) a brief description of the circumstances.

The above information should be kept in a separate book, or
alternatively, photocopies of form F2508 would be sufficient.

You should also report any accidents to yourself, as this may be
beneficial at a later stage.

Further details and guidance may be obtained from booklet
HS(R)23.

Trading Standards Department

The Trading Standards Department used to be known as 'Weights &
Measures'. Over the years it has grown tremendously and is now
responsible for enforcing the following Acts. If you think any of these
may affect you, please contact your local office to find out the latest
legislation. In some areas the department may be called the 'Consumer
Protection Department' or 'Consumer Services Dept.'

AGRICULTURE ACT 1970 Concerned with animal feeding stuffs
and fertilizers.

BRITISH TELECOMMUNICATIONS ACT 1981   All telephones and ancillary equipment have to be marked with a green triangle if they have been approved by BT or a red dot if they have not been approved.

CONSUMER CREDIT ACT 1974   If you wish to give credit in any form e.g. loans, HP etc you have to be licensed by the Office of Fair Trading.

CONSUMER PROTECTION ACT 1961 and 1971 and CONSUMER SAFETY ACT 1978   Concerned with basic safety for consumers e.g. baby dummies, prams, toys, bikes, inflammable nightwear, electrical goods, gas fires, etc etc.

DEVELOPMENT OF TOURISM ACT 1969   If you have more than 4 letting bedrooms or 8 beds, you have to display a price list in a conspicuous place.

ESTATE AGENTS ACT 1979   Concerned with safeguarding of deposits, fees, etc.

EXPLOSIVES ACTS 1875 and 1923   Safe storage of fireworks etc.

EXPLOSIVES (Age of Purchase etc.) ACT 1976

FABRICS (Misdescription) ACT 1913

FAIR TRADING ACT 1973

FOOD ACT 1984   Composition and labelling.

HALLMARKING ACT 1973   All items of gold, silver or platinum above a certain minimum weight have to be hallmarked, and a notice displayed close by indicating what the marks mean.

HEALTH & SAFETY at WORK etc. ACT 1974

MEDICINES ACT 1968   To do with adding medicines to animal feeds.

POISONS ACT 1972   A licence is needed to sell poisons. As an example, some hair colorants and disinfectants contain poison, also weedkillers etc.

PRICES ACTS 1974 and 1975   Each item for sale has to have a price on it, or close by.

TRADE DESCRIPTIONS ACTS 1968, 1972   An offence is committed if a member of the public is GENUINELY misled, or if a claim is proved false.

WEIGHTS & MEASURES ACT 1985   Concerned with all apparatus for use in trade, e.g. scales, petrol pumps, optics, glasses in pubs, prepacking apparatus. In fact any goods which are sold by reference to quantity, whether prepacked or loose.

PART 6

Reference Section

Small Firms Service

The Small Firms Service is run by the Department of Trade and Industry and can be of great help to anyone thinking of buying a shop, as well as to those who already run a business. They produce a series of useful free booklets, and can be contacted on the telephone by dialling 100 and asking for Freefone 2444. If you wish to visit one of their Centres for advice, it is advisable to telephone the Freefone number first, because some Centres are due to be re-located. If you wish, you may write to the address below instead:

Small Firms Division
Department of Trade and Industry
Ashdown House
123 Victoria Street
London SW1E 6RB

The Manpower Services Commission

The Manpower Services Commission will give details of various courses and schemes available. Look in your local telephone directory for the number to ring, or call in at your nearest Job Centre.

College Courses

College Courses leading to Diplomas and Certificates are offered by the College for the Distributive Trades, 30 Leicester Square, London WC2H 7LE. Tel. 01 839 1547. Details of courses available and entry requirements may be obtained from the college.

Colleges of Further Education

Colleges of Further Education sometimes offer various courses and seminars which may prove useful. Contact those within easy distance and ask for details.

Voluntary Associations

The Head Office of many of the Voluntary Associations is given below.

APT
Booker Belmont Wholesale Ltd., York House, Belmont Road, Uxbridge, Middx. Tel. 0895 38250.

BOB Group Ltd
Norwich Road, Mendlesham, Nr. Stowmarket, Suffolk, IP14 58A. Tel. 04494 381/2.

Fotovalue
276 Chase Road, Southgate, London N14 6HA. Tel. 01 882 2011.

Group Five (Shoes) Ltd
H Underwood and Sons Ltd., Hadleigh Road Industrial Estate, Ipswich, Suffolk. Tel. 0473 219955.

Hardware House
Kings Road, Flitwick, Bedford, MK45 1EH. Tel. 0525 712121.

Londis
Eurogroup House, 67/71 High Street, Hampton Hill, Middx. TW12 1LZ. Tel. 01 941 0344.

Mace Line
Gerrards House, Station Road, Gerrards Cross, Bucks, SL9 8HW. Tel. 0753 887355.

Spar (UK)
32-40 Headstone Drive, Harrow, Middx. HA3 5QT. Tel. 01 863 5511.

Maid Marian
Danish Bacon, Howardsgate, Welwyn Garden City, Herts. Tel. 07073 23421.

Target Food Group
70a The Centre, Highfield Road, Feltham, Middx. TW13 4BH. Tel. 01 890 0974.

N.I.S.A. Ltd
(National Independent Supermarkets Association) PO Box 45, Rotherham, S60 5BY. Tel. 0709 782589.

Numark Chemist Group
51 Boreham Road, Warminster, Wilts. BA12 9JU. Tel. 0985 215555.

Topdec
(wallpaper, paint etc.) PGW Holdings Ltd., Chilton House, Station Road, Chesham, Bucks. Tel 0494 774311.

Trend Voluntary Group Services Ltd
(paint, DIY etc.) 131a Bowes Rd., London, N13. Tel. 01 888 5891.

Unichem
(chemists) Cox Lane, Chessington, Surrey. Tel 01 391 2323.

Vantage Chemists
West Lane, Runcorn, Cheshire, WA7 2PE. Tel. 0928 717070.

Some More Useful Addresses

Association of Certified & Corporate Accountants
22 Bedford Square, London WC13 3HS.

Association of British Chambers of Commerce
6-14 Dean Farrar Street, London SW1H 0DX.

British Insurance Brokers' Association
Fountain House, 130 Fenchurch Street, London EC3M 5DJ. Tel. 01 623 9043.

Business Education Council
76 Portland Place, London W1.

Council for Small Industries in Rural Areas (COSIRA)
141 Castle Street, Salisbury, Wilts. SP1 3TP. Tel. (0722) 336255.

Department of Employment
22 St James's Square, London SW1 4JB.

Institute of Chartered Accountants
Moorgate Place, London EC2P 2BJ. Tel. 01 628 7060.

Royal Institute of Chartered Surveyors
12 Great George Street, Parliament Square, London SW1P 3AD.

Society of Company and Commercial Accountants
11 Portland Road, Edgbaston, Birmingham, B16 9HN.

Office of Fair Trading
Field House, 15/25 Breams Buildings, London EC4 1PR. Tel. 01 242 2858.

Law Society
113 Chancery Lane, London W1. Tel. 01 242 1222.

Royal Institute of British Architects
66 Portland Place, London W1N 4AB. Tel. 01 580 5533.

Trade Associations

There follows a list of the main Trade Associations, many of which produce a trade journal. These can provide some valuable sources of information.

Amalgamated Master Diarymen Ltd
   Bradford & Bingley House, 220 Hoe Street, London E17 3AY.
   Tel. 01 521 8855.

Association of British Laundry, Cleaning & Rental Services Ltd
   Lancaster Gate House, 319 Pinner Road, Harrow.
   Tel. 01 863 7755.

Association Of Independent Retailers
   Newton Road, Worcester WR5 1JX. Tel. 0905 28165.

Bakery Allied Traders Association Ltd
   6 Catherine Street, London WC2B 5JJ. Tel. 01 836 2460.

Bookmakers Association
   22 Malthouse Lane, Birmingham, B8. Tel. 021 327 3031.

Booksellers Association of Great Britain and Ireland
   154 Buckingham Palace Road, London SW1W 9TZ.
   Tel. 01 730 8214.

British Antique Dealers Association
   20 Rutland Gate, London SW7 1BD. Tel. 01 589 4128.

British Franchise Association
   Franchise Chambers, 75a Bell Street, Henley on Thames, Oxon.
   Tel. 0491 578049.

British Fur Trade Association
   68 Upper Thames Street, London EC4V 3AN. Tel. 01 248 5947.

British Hardware Federation
   20 Harborne Rd, Edgbaston, Birmingham B15 3AB.
   Tel. 021 454 4385.

British Hotels, Restaurants and Caterers Association
   40 Duke Street, London W1M 6HR. Tel. 01 499 6641.

British Independent Grocers Association (BIGA)
   Federation House, 17 Farnborough Street, Farnborough, Hants.
   GU14 8AG (F515001)

British Jewellery & Giftware Federation
   27 Frederick Street, Birmingham B1 3HJ. Tel. 021 236 2657.

British Retailers Association
Commonwealth House, 1/19 New Oxford Street, London WC1A
1PA. Tel. 01 404 0955.

Consumer Credit Association of the United Kingdom
Queens House, Queens Road, Chester CH1 3BQ.
Tel. 0244 312044.

Consumer Credit Trade Association
3 Berners Street, London W1P 3AG. Tel. 01 636 7564.

Delicatessen and Fine Food Association
3 Fairfield Avenue, Staines, Middx. TW18 4AB. Tel. 0784 61339.

Drapers' Chamber of Trade
North Bar, Banbury, Oxon. Tel. 0295 53601.

Federation of Sports Goods Distributors Ltd
7 Pelham Road, Lindfield, Haywards Heath, Sussex RH16 2EW.
Tel. 04447 3769.

Food and Drink Federation
6 Catherine Street, London WC2 5JJ. Tel. 01 836 2460.

Footwear Distributors' Federation
Commonwealth House, 1/19 New Oxford Street, London WC1A
1PA. Tel. 01 404 0955.

Horticultural Trades Association
19 High St, Theale, Reading, Berks RG7 5AH. Tel. 0734 303132.

Independent Footwear Retailers Association
3 Masons Avenue, Wealdstone, Harrow HA3 5AH.
Tel. 01 427 1545.

Institute of Meat
Boundary House, 91/93 Charterhouse Street, London EC1M 6HR.
Tel. 01 253 2971.

London Fish & Poultry Retailers Association
66 Aberdour Rd, Goodmayes, Essex IG3 9PG. Tel. 01 590 4200.

Menswear Association of Britain Ltd
Palladium House, 1-4 Argyll St, London W1V 2HR.
Tel. 01 734 6865.

Music Trades Association
PO Box 249, London W4 5EX. Tel. 01 994 7592.

National Association of Cycle & Motor Cycle Traders Ltd
31a High St, Tunbridge Wells, Kent TN1 1XN. Tel. 0892 26081.

National Association of Health Stores
Byron House, 1 College St, Nottingham, Notts. NG1 5AQ.
Tel. 0602 474165.

National Association of Master Bakers, Confectioners & Caterers
50 Alexandra Rd, Wimbledon SW19 7BR. Tel. 01 947 7781.

National Association of Retail Furnishers
17-21 George St, Croydon CR9 1TQ. Tel. 01 680 8444.

National Association of Shopfitters
NAS House, 411 Limpsfield Rd, The Green, Warlingham, Surrey
CR3 9HA. Tel. 088 32 4961.

National Association of Shopkeepers
Lynch House, 91 Mansfield Rd, Nottingham, Notts NG1 3FN.
Tel. 0602 475046.

National Association of Toy Retailers
20 Knave Wood Rd, Kemsing, Sevenoaks, Kent.

National Chamber of Trade
Enterprise House, Henley on Thames, Oxon. RG9 1TU.
Tel. 0491 576161.

National Federation of Fish Friers
Federation House, 289 Dewsbury Rd, Leeds LS11 5HW.
Tel. 0532 713291.

National Federation of Fishmongers Ltd
Queensway House, 2 Queensway, Redhill, Surrey RH1 1QS.
Tel. Redhill 68611.

National Federation of Meat Traders
1 Belgrove, Tunbridge Wells, Kent.

National Federation of Retail Newsagents
2 Bridewell Place, London EC4V 6AR. Tel. 01 353 6816.

National Federation of Subpostmasters
Evelyn House, 22 Windlesham Gdns, Shoreham by Sea BN4 5AZ.
Tel. 07917 2324.

National Hairdressers Federation
11 Goldington Rd, Bedford MK40 3JY. Tel. 0234 60332.

National Institute of Hardware
10 Leam Terrace, Leamington Spa. Tel. Leamington Spa 21284.

The National Pharmaceutical Association Ltd
Mallinson House, 40-42 St. Peter's St, St Albans, Herts. AL1 3NP.
Tel. 0727 32161.

National Union of Licensed Victuallers
2 Downing St, Farnham, Surrey GU9 7NX. Tel. 0252 714448.

Office Machines & Equipment Federation
16 Wood St, Kingston-upon-Thames, Surrey KT1 1UE.
Tel. 01 549 7699.

The Pet Trade Association Ltd
151 Pampisford Rd, South Croydon, Surrey CR2 6DE.
Tel. 01 681 3708.

Radio, Electrical & Television Retailers Association
Retra House, 57-61 Newington Causeway, London SE1 6BE.
Tel. 01 403 1463.

Retail Confectioners & Tobacconists Association Ltd.
Ashley House, 53 Christchurch Ave, London N12 0DH.
Tel. 01 445 6344.

Retail Fruit Trade Federation
108/110 Market Towers, Nine Elms Lane, London SW8 5NS.
Tel. 01 720 9168.

Shop & Display Equipment Association
24 Croydon Rd, Caterham, Surrey CR3 6YR. Tel. 0883 48911.

Society of Master Shoe Repairers
St. Crispin's House, 21 Station Rd, Desborough, Northants
NN14 25A. Tel. 0536 760374.

Wallpaper, Paint & Wallcovering Retailers Association
PO Box 44, Walsall, West Midlands. Tel. 0922 31134.

Trade Journals

As well as journals published by Trade Associations there are a
multitude of others that can be obtained from your newsagent. Some
of these are listed below. There are also a number of free magazines
available to those already in business.

Antiques Trade Gazette	The Grocer
Bookseller	Hairdressers Journal
Caterer and Hotelkeeper	International
Chemist and Druggist	Hardware Trade Journal
Drapers' Record	Meat Trades Journal
CTN/Confectioner, Tobacconist	Newsagent
& Confectioner	Painting and Decorating Journal
Fast Foodservice	Retail Newsagent Tobacconist &
Fish Trader	Confectioner
Fruit Trades Journal	Shoe and Leather News
	Video Retailer

If you wish to find out the names of all the available journals, or if you have a particular trade in mind and do not know if there is a journal for it, I recommend a trip to your local reference library and a browse through a book called BRAD (British Rate & Data) which lists all types of current publications and their advertising rates.

Your local reference library is another valuable source of information for all types of queries — do not be afraid to make use of it.

Index